WITHDRAWN
NDSU

PATTERNS IN THACKERAY'S FICTION

PATTERNS IN THACKERAY'S FICTION

James H. Wheatley

THE M.I.T. PRESS
MASSACHUSETTS INSTITUTE OF TECHNOLOGY
CAMBRIDGE, MASSACHUSETTS, AND LONDON, ENGLAND

220821

Copyright © 1969 by
The Massachusetts Institute of Technology

Set in Photon Baskerville
Printed and bound in the United States of America

Designed by Dwight E. Agner

All rights reserved. No part of this book may be reproduced or utilized in any form or by any means, electronic or mechanical, including photocopying, recording, or by any information storage and retrieval system, without permission in writing from the publisher.

Library of Congress catalog card number: 69–19245

To My Wife

Louise Stevens Wheatley

CONTENTS

CONTENTS

ACKNOWLEDGMENTS

The list of colleagues and friends who have generously and helpfully read manuscript versions of this book is too long to include here, but I cannot omit thanking especially Robert Gorham Davis, Louis Kampf, John Lynen, Richard Ohmann, and Paul Smith. I must also thank the University of Illinois for a Summer Research Grant, and Wesleyan University for funds for research and typing.

JAMES H. WHEATLEY

Glastonbury, Connecticut
August 1968

INTRODUCTION

IN HISTORY AND OUT

To define the art of Thackeray so that discussion neither moves too quickly from the novels into biography or philosophy nor is confined too narrowly in novelistic technique is a reasonable, but difficult and intriguing, goal. Thackeray's particular kind of art seems to have the power to entice inadequate commentary and then, disconcertingly, to show it up as one-sided or truncated or misleading in some way. The narrator's voice is one such enticement, leading to speculation on the man behind the pen, the name under the nom de plume, and on the value of the "timeless truths" the narrator recommends. Ultimately, of course, we must engage these questions if we take art seriously, but the problem is to decide how soon, and how directly, that engagement should take place. Similarly, the brilliance of his virtuosity, the apparent ease with which he manipulates whole matrices of storytelling conventions, is another enticement, tempting us to restrict our gaze to this facet or perhaps to look for the birth of the modern novel in his pages.

Even more tempting is the possibility of setting Thackeray firmly in his own time, with the risk of immersing him in it completely. Kathleen Tillotson has performed a valuable service in showing how close the relations were between novelists and the reading public of the 1840's,[1] especially because the practice of serial publication facilitated "feedback" from the audience to the novel in progress. A good many of Thackeray's most basic attitudes—his seriousness and playfulness, his certainties and evasions—seem most at home in England in the fifteen or twenty years from about 1830 to the middle or late 1840's. As he himself came to feel, he had outlived his times when he died in 1863, at the age of fifty-two, and though several strands contributed to that feeling, one of them was surely that a new generation had arrived and was impatient with his. Despite Thackeray's personal and artistic development, his social attitudes and intellectual concerns remain those of the 1830's and early 1840's. The intellectual ferment of the 1850's was being prepared in the forties by such books as John Stuart Mill's *System of Logic* (1843) and George Eliot's translation of David Strauss' *Das Leben Jesu* (1846). But we can hardly imagine Thackeray reading Mill, much less becoming excited if he did, and as for Strauss and the higher criticism of the Bible, we can only imagine Thackeray saying, like George Eliot's Mr. Brooke, "I went into [that] a great deal myself at one time; but I saw it would not do."[2]

More than temperament seems to contribute to Thackeray's apparent inertia: In the ten years between 1846 and 1856, his public position changed from being considered avant-garde, almost the intellectual's answer to Charles Dickens, to passé. It was not simply that he had taken to repeating himself in *The Virginians* and *The Adventures of Philip,* but that what he repeated could only seem a dead end: a troubled acceptance of the world that afforded few identifiable components and few directions for development to the more intellectual younger generation.

Whole attitudes that had been implicit and acceptable—implicit partly because they were acceptable—were now beginning to have names and with names, attackers and defenders. He could protest, at a slur against his position, that his works had been written "by a God-loving man" whose morality was "the teaching Domini Nostri,"[3] but it was a Christianity suited to 1845, not 1855. In his last years, Thackeray sometimes seems to be a man blinking in the sudden light. "I admire but cant read Adam Bede and the books of that Author," he said in 1861.[4]

To have come from a family with strong roots in the upper middle class, to have gone to the famous Charterhouse School and then on to Cambridge, not Oxford, and to have begun to think and produce in the 1830's—all these factors meant that one knew, for instance, how Seriousness looked and felt, and how important it was, even when one chose not to be Serious, or could not measure up. We hear of Thackeray going with his earnestly religious friend, John Allen, to a sermon at Cambridge in 1830, when Robert Evans, a Fellow and Tutor of Trinity College, symbolically preached "against Systems of Morality."[5] The official method of philosophizing was still that of the Common Sense school, a way of formulating, as Noel Annan says, "the moral platitudes of the club and coffee-house."[6] Intuition was the basis of Christian apologetics, and intuition not only did not require but might be positively weakened by too much thinking. Toward morals the same attitude existed. Thackeray records in his diary for 1832 reading Goethe's *Wilhelm Meister,* "and a wretched performance I thought it. . . . Neither delicacy morality or philosophy as I thought, but not being initiated have perhaps no business to judge of the latter—of the two former most people are competent judges . . ."[7]

For the group that came out of Cambridge in Thackeray's generation, there would never be any of Oxford's "impossible loyalties," no intellectual fervor. Carlyle would seem perhaps too narrow and shrill, but was obviously a great man and on the right track, fighting systems of morality with what seemed to be facts of experience, such as Duty. "Narrowness," in fact, would be a key critical term, useful in part because it was so mild, the hallmark of minds that worked by inclusion rather than exclusion. For Thackeray, the Evangelical Christianity to which his mother subscribed was too narrow—not merely wrong here or there, although he thought it that, but narrow—and tending to produce narrowness in its adherents. Christ, he thought, taught love, not narrowness.[8]

"We are of the Clapham Theology," he wrote half-seriously in 1851, warning a Roman Catholic governess against proselytizing his daughters.[9] In the sense in which he meant it, much of middle-class England was of the Clapham Religion. Its original orthodoxy was weakened or gone, but many of the attitudes of that evangelical group were as strong as ever and were now widely accepted. Noel Annan, in his brilliant biography of Thackeray's son-in-law, Leslie Stephen, has demonstrated the spiritual connections between members of the original "Clapham Sect," as they were at first derisively called, and their literal descendants, reaching down to the Bloomsbury group of this century. Thackeray is a descendant by adoption and milieu. Annan writes of Stephen: "The peremptory demand for sincerity, the delight in plain-speaking, the unvarying accent on conduct, and the conviction that he who has attained a Higher Truth must himself evangelize, leap from the pages of Stephen's books and proclaim him a child of the Evangelical tradition."[10] Leslie Stephen went up to Cambridge twenty-one years after Thackeray, read Mill as an undergraduate, and became a "Rationalist," a militant agnostic; Thackeray wrote that during his grave illness in 1849, facing death, he had been "as easy in mind and as trustful of God and as confident in his wisdom & mercy" as any saint—or clergyman.[11] The two men are strikingly similar in background. Although the form and extent of Thackeray's rebellion against that background, and his transformation of it, differ widely from Stephen's, the difference seems as much a matter of the twenty years between their arrival at Cambridge as it does a matter of talent or temperament. Had Thackeray been highly intellectual by nature, the age would have provided no models or outlets likely to interest one of his class and education.

Instead, he was only—and here even so brief a summary may suggest the limits of the cultural history of literature—a mere artist, although a very intelligent one indeed. More intelligent, we must say, than Dickens, in the usual senses of "intelligent." If we ask, as the Dickensians are likely to do, whether Thackeray is as psychologically interesting, and especially whether his unconscious self was as powerful and "articulate" as was Dickens', the answer to at least the latter question must be no. (The only extended attempt to locate Thackeray's unconscious life disapproves of what it finds.)[12] Yet if Dickens was in his generation the poet of the Id and Superego, Thackeray was the poet of the Ego: of the self scrutinizing itself, retaining as much pleasure and internalized authority as is consonant with its own existence, yet willing to imagine giving that up, too; carefully noting the shocks and shifts of triumph and defeat, concession and accession. For that activity, he makes us feel, is the *life* of the ego, as opposed to its occasional and more lurid aggressive raids in defense of its life.

His letters show him constructing a fiercely impregnable

ego's world—liberal in politics, neo-Claphamite in religion, middle class in loyalty—and backing off from it, playing with it, keeping it in motion. He is the world he sees, poor lucky man, and that is what his art ultimately displays.

THE ARGUMENT FROM PARODY

When Sir Max Beerbohm read Thackeray as a boy, the experience gave him "all unconsciously a feeling for how English could be written."[13] The connections between the two men are intriguing. Fifty years apart, they attended the same school, Charterhouse, which Addison and Steele had attended before them. Thackeray began his literary career as a parodist, a fact not unusual in itself, as so many writers have begun their careers this way. It takes on significance, however, when we consider not only how central to all of Thackeray's career the art of parody is, but also to what heights the nineteenth century, and especially Beerbohm, carried the art. When Thackeray's popularity declined early in the twentieth century, the heyday of parody was over, and Beerbohm had retired from active writing. Yet a history of the art might show that it had deep connections with the aesthetic movement of the 1890's, and that it went underground only to flower, all changed, in the work of T. S. Eliot, Ezra Pound, and James Joyce.

The reasons for the vitality of parody are not far to seek. It is funny, and in as many ways as other jokes can be, from the bitter to the preposterous. It differs from other jokes in being literary, and in order for it to be so the writer makes a curious assumption, which must seem all the more curious to those who think that literature is the outpouring of the heart. For in writing a parody, the author assumes that there is a profound connection between the language a man uses and his way of thinking about himself and the world. Outpourings, the parodist might say, depend for their authenticity as much on form as they do on sincerity. To the good parodist—one who is not simply burlesquing external tricks of speech—a mode of language is a mode of thought, and this assumption provides him with his materials. There may be other assumptions (as we shall have to consider when we take up Thackeray's early parodies), but for good parody this is the *sine qua non*.

One implication of this view of parody—let us call it that of True Parody—is that the writer is relatively conscious of this assumption. His "ear for language" is an ear for what men are thinking and feeling when they use language in a certain way; it is a heightened sensitivity to the ways in which language mirrors, or can be seen to mirror, perception. The good parodist practices on a large and casual scale what the "new critics" of this century have preached and analyzed in their scrutiny of the interdependence of "form" and "content" in literature.

A certain kind of parody could be written on the basis of the classical theory of levels of style (high, middle, and low) and of the need for decorum: divergence from some assumed norm might seem sufficient cause for laughter and produce a kind of rudimentary parody. Those norms, together with a far more complicated one, the notion of "a language of good sense," have combined to produce much of the parody in Swift and Pope. But Thackeray and Beerbohm go far beyond anything available to the eighteenth-century wits. They were freer, more conscious of wealth and variety in the world, more conscious of exactly what they were doing. Perhaps they were more self-conscious because, to put it the other way around, the notions of there being only a few levels of language, of the necessity for decorum, and of the existence of a language of good sense were all no longer available to them.

When Thackeray died, Carlyle called him the best stylist of the generation;[14] and it was a generation, we are beginning to see, which took style very seriously. Mid-Victorians meant things by the word style, saw things by means of it, and used styles themselves in ways difficult for us to recover now. Whatever Carlyle meant by his statement, he certainly did not mean that he thought Thackeray the greatest writer of his generation, nor was he recommending imitation of Thackeray's style. Carlyle probably meant that Thackeray had *used* style more fully and successfully than any other writer of the age. Today, to make the claim that Thackeray's greatness lies in his style is to risk damning him with very faint praise, and yet that is one of the claims this book will make. In order to see it as high praise, we need to find ways of stating explicitly much of what Carlyle and his generation could take for granted, as well as to extend their positions.

The nature and value of Thackeray's art are not, of course, reducible to the limits of parody. But the argument that his art derives from parody seems a useful beginning because, if our description of True Parody is accurate, it may help to isolate a certain kind of consciousness, certain kinds of sophistication, which are central to his art. Parody, I shall argue, is both conceptually and biographically fundamental to Thackeray's career as a novelist.

In what follows, I have tried to keep two schemes at work, superimposing one on the other: first, that of a literary biography, recording the triumphs, experiments, and progressions of a fertile and developing artist; second, that of a literary anatomy, discussing matters central to his art as a whole.

In pursuing both schemes, it has seemed wise to restrict discussion to his major fiction as the central area of concern, treating lesser works or subsidiary genres only by implication or in those cases, such as the early work dealt with in the first two chapters, when the relative slightness of the fiction is a positive aid in isolating certain of his concerns. He also wrote light verse, travel books, stories for the Christmas trade, and above all essays and reviews. For certain readers his essays, especially the "Roundabout Papers" written late in life for *The Cornhill Magazine,* provide the quintessential Thackeray. For such readers—and they do not belong in quite the same category with those who prefer Keats' letters to his poems—I hope that what is said about the fiction will seem applicable to the essays.

The danger in pursuing two schemes—the chronological and the analytic—is that neither scheme may work, that the reader will never find everything relevant to a work treated where he thinks it ought to be. But the gains, I hope, will be real ones. Thackeray's career as a writer does not contain sudden shifts, is always multifaceted, and many of the facets are constant; but real developments do occur. Chronologically, three main periods can be distinguished: the early work through *The Book of Snobs* (1846–1847); *Vanity Fair* (1847–1848), all by itself; and the three following novels *(Pendennis, Henry Esmond,* and *The Newcomes),* filled out by their successors, *The Virginians* and *The Adventures of Philip.* Here the chapters follow that division. Analytically, the first two chapters examine Thackeray's uses and extensions of parody; the next two chapters try to define various kinds of structural patterns and their thematic implications in *Vanity Fair,* based on the earlier discussion; and the last two chapters trace extensions of these problems in the later novels, finally approaching by this route the vexed and intriguing problem of realism in his fiction. The argument ought to accumulate: if I have succeeded, the *Vanity Fair* chapters will seem relevant to his later work, the later chapters relevant, if not as naturally applicable, to *Vanity Fair.*

Chapter One

EARLY PARODY

"THE PROFESSOR"

In this early piece of short fiction, Thackeray already shows an extraordinary sophistication. Written for *Fraser's* and published in 1837, it is a complex little piece in two chapters, made up of several different kinds of jokes. It is surprising how well they all fit together: there is more than an apprentice ability in the style, which by its management of modulations and intermixtures makes the story still enjoyable.

Of the large elements that can be isolated, there is, first, the story of a successful mountebank, Dando the Oyster Eater, who wins the affection of an oysterman's daughter, Adeliza Grampus. Both are playing two roles: he, by succeeding in being hired to teach at a girls' school as Professor Dandola, teacher of dancing and of the "new amusement," gymnastics, and by pretending that he is "really" Roderick, or Ferdinand—or Roderick Ferdinand—last of the noble house of Dandola; she, by pretending to be a young aristocrat, and conceiving herself to be the heroine in a world in which a mysterious stranger turns out to be "36th Count of Dandola" and in love with her. There is such a world, of course, in the romances that are the main target of the parody, but it is not "our" world. As though to testify to its reality—and basic unreality—Adeliza falls in a dead faint when she realizes the truth about her lover, and rises from that trance "a MANIAC!"

Unlike the modern "sick" joke, which deliberately violates a conventional moral order, or the merely callous joke, this is a highly sophisticated socioliterary one, depending on the play among various levels of reality and illusion. And, like many good jokes, this one is curative. It takes the casual notion that language is somehow the mirror of truth and nature—a notion on which good and bad art both depend—and refines it. Highflown language need not mirror anything "real" at all, for it can be learned from the silly romances of such contemporary favorites as "LEL" and Bulwer Lytton. In fact, the chances are slight that language mirrors anything but itself, and are good that it is pretentious in both senses, that is, self-congratulatory and deceptive.

The subtitle announces "A Tale of Sentiment," complete with "poetic" epigraph ("Why, then, the World's mine oyster"). The narrator himself is playing the role of the romancer, who intersperses his account of this "pathetic occurrence" with moral banalities supported by slightly melodramatic rhythms: "The reader will gather from this, that Dandola's after-conduct at Miss Pidge's was not satisfactory, nor was it; and may every mistress of such an establishment remember that confidence can be sometimes misplaced; that friendship is frequently but another name for villainy. But to our story."[1] Such a passage is sonic melodrama because it depends so heavily on the contrast between the orotund sound of the narrator's reflective digression and its banal content. The reader soon learns to listen for and treasure such self-important pronouncements, and is rewarded here by the additional richness of the narrator's solemnly resuming his "real" task: "But to our story."

Although the narrator is so much a part of the game, the "reality" that breaks in to deflate these pretensions is fairly simple and clear. The most obvious device is the dropped *h* in the midst of a character's soaring effusion, but Thackeray finds a way to freshen even this: "Although the Signor's name was decidedly foreign, so English was his appearance, and so entirely did he disguise his accent, that it was impossible to tell of what place he was a native, if not of London, and of the very heart of it; for he had caught completely the peculiarities which distinguish the so-called cockney part of the City, and obliterated his *h*'s and doubled his *v*'s, as if he had been for all his life in the neighborhood of Bow bells."[2] Evidently the possibility that the Signor really is a Cockney is too simple, direct, and plausible to occur to the narrator.

At times slang, or a slight bluntness of diction, interrupts the smooth flow of pretentiousness and plunges us into bathos: "Her father had sent her from home at fifteen [to school], because she had fallen in love with the young man who opened natives in the shop, and had vowed to slay herself with the oyster-knife . . ."[3] If only, the devoted reader of contemporary romances might ask, the young man's job were left unspecified, or at least he were allowed to open oysters in general; but failing even that much decorum, "native oysters" would be a little better than "natives" alone. It would help to prevent the incursion of a world in which food is casually sold and consumed, sometimes with pleasure; and it might also help a little, by deflecting attention, to exclude the painful suggestion of a world in which boys work their way up some stratified economic ladder from humbler to more significant tasks. And what, after all, could be the top of this ladder? Opening lobsters? As for that oyster-knife: no, nobody could "slay" herself with such a device.

Practicing his amatory wiles during a dancing lesson, Dandola "gently seizes her hand, he raises it considerably above the level of her ear, he places the tips of his left-hand fingers gently upon the young lady's spine, and in this seducing attitude gazes tenderly into her eyes!" Again, explicit physical details "spoil" the scene, producing the same effect as sudden airpockets on a smooth flight followed by soaring thermal updrafts. The passage just quoted rises to a positive crescendo:

> . . . gazes tenderly into her eyes! I say that no woman at any age can stand this attitude and this look especially when darted from such eyes as those of Dandola. On the first two occasions when the adventurer attempted this audacious manoeuver, his victim blushed only, and trembled; on the third she dropped her full eyelids and turned ghastly pale. "A glass of water," cried Adeliza, "or I faint." The dancing-master hastened eagerly away to procure the desired beverage, and, as he put it to her lips, whispered thrillingly in her ear, "Thine, thine for ever, Adeliza!"[4]

This exaggeration implies both a linguistic and a moral standard: there must be, somewhere, a language of good sense, in which water is not called "the desired beverage"; and there also must be such a thing as sensible behavior, in which one does not get carried away so far by so little. Both standards are happily violated in a sentence like " 'A glass of water,' cried Adeliza, 'or I faint.' " The narrator has placed his "cried Adeliza" for maximum melodramatic effect, and it corresponds perfectly to the girl's gasping pause before she announces heroically the possible effect of so literary a passion.

There are some hints of what the more realistic grounds of sentiment would be, and these are chiefly of two sorts. One, a kind of playful sexuality, perhaps meant to be appropriate to the lower orders, underlies and comments on the unreality of romantic love conventions. Dando's passion for oysters, according to a different kind of convention, makes him "a general lover of the sex" because oysters have long been supposed to be aphrodisiac. The narrator glances at this joke obliquely in his mock summation: "If [my tale] may have taught . . . to manhood the crime, the *meanness* of gluttony, the vice which it occasions, and the wicked passions it fosters . . . the writer seeks for no other reward."[5] Mrs. Grampus, the novel-reading mother who gave Adeliza her incongruous first name, lives in a "real" world of oysters and stolen "busses": a scene which the narrator only overhears from the next room of the shop is explicit enough. Mrs. Grampus has overheard "a scuffle, a giggle and a smack" in the room where Adeliza is serving Dando, and takes in the lobster herself. " 'For shame, sir!' said she solemnly; but all of a sudden she began to giggle like her daughter, and her speech ended with an *'Have done now!'* . . . Mrs. Grampus returned to the shop, rubbing her lips with her fat arms, and restored to perfect good-humour."[6] The method of overhearing is not of course prurient, for the main point to be made is the foolishness of Adeliza's humorless poses, compared to the "good-humour" of an occasional scuffle with a waitress.

There are also some suggestions, hardly developed, of a standard of sympathy that is violated by the mistreatment of Miss Pidge and the apprentice boy at the shop. Miss Pidge got Dando his job at the school, but he callously dismisses his debt to her in his explanation to Adeliza, who notices no cruelty. In fact, Thackeray shows, the mock humility of a romance heroine hides a great deal of arrogance. " 'Oh, Binx!' would Adeliza continue, 'is it not passing strange that one of that mighty ducal race should have lived to this day, and live to love *me?* But I, too,' Adeliza would add archly, 'am, as you know, a daughter of the sea.' "[7] So when she steals money from her father's till in order to support Dando, and the apprentice is accused of her theft and convicted, her only comment in a letter to Dando is this: "A sudden thought! Our apprentice is dismissed. My father dines abroad; I shall be in the retail establishment all the night, *alone*."[8]

But Miss Pidge, the other victim, is a novel reader herself, and so her misfortunes, even when she loses her school because of the scandal, cannot be very real: " 'I knew it! I knew it! . . . he told me that none ever prospered who loved him—that every flower was blighted upon which he shone! Ferdinand! Ferdinand, you have caused ruin there! (pointing to the empty cupboards and forms); but what is that to the blacker ruin *here?*' and the poor creature slapped her heart, and the big tears rolled down her chin, and so into her tucker."[9] These are merely suggestions of a standard of sympathy as one coordinate of reality, for the story is finally about language, not life, or rather, it is about the relations between a certain kind of language and life. But this concern is what makes it more than a simple parody of romances. Thackeray has not simply applied the language of an author to incongruous material in the way a parodist might record in Jamesian style a visit to a Chinese laundry. He has imagined a world in which Chinese launderers read James, and try to think, act, and talk like characters from his books. That would be a mode of living created by language, as Adeliza's is. It would also be a kind of madness, as their language would have become divorced from so much of life; and in "The Professor," language breaks raucously free, when Adeliza becomes "a MANIAC!" Maniacs only occur in romances, fortunately, so we need only register our approval at so doubly appropriate an outcome.

Harry Levin has said that most writers pass through parody, progress "from the imitation of art through parody to the imitation of nature."[10] But Thackeray has already moved, in this early story, beyond the initial stage: he is making parody work for him, putting it in the service, as he would say, of "truth and nature."

The coordinates of truth and nature, of the story's reality, we have seen to be primarily social and economic. The "good sense" that recognizes reality recognizes "natural" distinctions of rank and money. These distinctions make possible the notion of a language of good sense: they are the grounds of the parody, the containing truth within which Thackeray's curiosity about and delight in language can operate. But his primary interest here, as we have seen, is in those modes of language which define a whole way of life, of conceiving the world. To put it another way, the socioeconomic "truth" contains the story but does not confine it. It is a certain sort of language that confines the world by rigidly systematizing it, as the careful mixture of modes of language makes clear: the bathos, for instance, "frees" the language as though inadvertently for a minute from the rigors of an absurd system by introducing anomalous "facts."

Freedom from system, openness, and especially an intellectual geniality and responsiveness, are thus characteristics of a posture of wisdom with which Thackeray began his career as comic writer. Parody was an effective means of attaining this posture; at the same time, it sensitized him to modes of perception as they are presented in language.

"NOVELS BY EMINENT HANDS"

In the ten years between "The Professor" and *Vanity Fair* (1848), Thackeray wrote a great deal and in a wide variety of forms.

Parody is related to everything he did in this period, but only at the end of it did he publish, in *Punch,* a series of "Prize Novels," later collected as "Novels by Eminent Hands," which specifically imitate the novels of some of his contemporaries. Before going back to explore the rich output of these years, we may conveniently use these late parodies to bracket the period. Although perhaps more finely drawn, in places, than "The Professor," they are technically less interesting and might be called "straight" parodies. They do show, however, several new kinds of emphasis.

The subject matter of each is a specific kind of novel, and Thackeray's general strategy is simple exaggeration in order to bring out the characteristics which he thinks central to each novelist. It is interesting that the characteristics on which he concentrates fall into two fairly clear categories: the character of the narrator, and what we may call the morality of his world view. Two exceptions are a partial parody of Thackeray's own *Yellowplush Papers* (1837–1838), and a "Plan" for a prize novel under which the author may earn extra money by planting, almost subliminally, advertisements for particular shops and products. In the others, with varying severity, Thackeray deals with the vanity of the narrators and the grotesqueries of their morals. Perhaps, as Gordon Ray suggests, Bulwer had more cause than the other authors parodied to wince,[11] but all had reason to feel themselves quite thoroughly attacked. Especially in an age that tended to see no distinction between the man and the voice and to take seriously edification in any form, and of whatever kind, Thackeray's parodies may well have seemed devastating.

The narrator of "George de Barnwell," by "Sir E. L. B. L. Bart.," is a pretentious fop, who ogles himself in the mirror of his own preposterous prose. In his own eyes, he is Bard,

Philosopher, Historian, Wit. His addresses to the reader are occasions for self-congratulation and self-pity: "Listen! I tell thee a tale—not of Kings—but of Men—not of Thrones, but of Love, and Grief, and Crime. Listen, and but once more. 'Tis for the last time (probably) these fingers shall sweep the strings."[12]

Fatally addicted to silly euphemisms and the cliché, the narrator's wit is sodden, his pathos preposterous, his history inaccurate, and his philosophy stupefying. He claims to be enamoured of the True and the Beautiful, terms not only "marriageable" ("In the Morning of Life the Truthful wooed the Beautiful, and their offspring was Love") but interchangeable with each other and with something called the Ideal. Together these four empty terms are the sanction for a kind of art that avoids specific detail while pretending to a "philosophical" overview of life:

> 'Twas noonday in Chepe. High Tide in the mighty River City!—its banks well-nigh over-flowing with the myriad-waved Stream of Man! . . . The imprecations of the charioteers were terrible. From the noble's broidered hammercloth, or the driving-seat of the common coach, each driver assailed the other with floods of ribald satire. . . . And the Philosopher, as he regarded the hot strife and struggle of these candidates in the race for Gold, thought with a sigh of the Truthful and the Beautiful, and walked on, melancholy and serene.[13]

The lack of detail—or rather, the ostensible detail that is made to dissolve into the terminology used to describe it—is paralleled by a social snobbery that dismisses most of mankind and its interests.

Even so long a catalogue of charges does not begin to exhaust the number of internally decorous touches by which Thackeray builds up a whole world view in this prose. But it is a world view of which emptiness is the identifying mark—one thinks of a balloon blown big by self-love. Nothing but language, a set of terministic postures, really exists. By this point in his career, Thackeray has not only been considering but collecting, as a connoisseur, what I call postures of wisdom.

The plot parallels the prose because, as in Bulwer's novel, *Eugene Aram,* a young man commits murder in pursuing The Ideal. His narrator must deplore, but cannot blame, so interesting a violation of The Real. To heighten the absurdity, Thackeray takes for his hero George Barnwell, from the old story of the London apprentice who robbed his employer's till and killed him. Here he is George de Barnwell; and he hides beneath his apron a heart so noble, and has wit and learning so profound, that he easily triumphs over Pope, Swift, Steele, Addison, and Bolingbroke, all of whom he encounters at Button's Coffeehouse. After the murder, the prison chaplain, Doctor Fizwig, is as his name implies no match for George's speculative eloquence: " 'Were it Crime, I should feel Remorse. Where there is no Remorse, Crime cannot exist. I am not sorry: therefore, I am innocent. Is the proposition a fair one?' The excellent Doctor admitted that it was not to be contested."[14] George gaily eats his last meal, secure in his knowledge that, like Socrates, Seneca, Brutus, and Cleopatra, he has played his "great Hazard" and, like them, is simply paying his "forfeit" to a vulgar world. But despite such cheerful stoicism, Dr. Fizwig, invited to share this last meal, "could scarcely eat it for tears."[15] The appeal to sympathy for such conceptual imprisonment evidently struck Thackeray as a serious matter, worth all the exposure he could manage. But it is hard not to feel that delight in such thoroughgoing decorum of language and thought did not play a major part in Thackeray's plan.

In the other parodies, he may have felt he had less to work with. Only one other—"Barbazure," which parodies the romances of G. P. R. James—has a complete plot, dependent on a simple last-minute rescue, and none has the inventive richness of the Bulwer parody. Thackeray's targets, however, are the same. For example, the parody of Disraeli, "Codlingsby," focuses on the curious mixture of dandiacal pretentiousness and earnest naïveté of its narrator. Toward the English aristocracy, personified by "Godfrey de Bouillon, Marquis of Codlingsby," the mock narrator exhibits a kind of fawning familiarity, dropping names and in-group data with an attempt at the careless exactness which he seems to reverence in that class. "He had been to take a box for Armida at Madame Vestris's theatre. That little Armida was *folle* of Madame Vestris's theatre; and her little brougham, and her little self . . . might be seen, three nights in the week at least, in the narrow, charming, comfortable little theatre. Godfrey had the box. He was strolling, listlessly, eastward . . ."[16]

But the narrator's admiration for the listless aristocracy is nothing compared to the chauvinism with which he regards Jews. They are beautiful, cultured, talented, and they secretly run the world. It is a benign conspiracy, however, responsible for the salvation of more than one government. Rafael Mendoza, unlike his counterpart Sidonia in Disraeli's novel, *Coningsby,* occasionally uses the disguise of an ignorant and crafty old-clothes dealer, but even his accent is a disguise and behind the greasy shop is a palatial residence.

The walls were hung with cloth of silver. . . . The hangings were overhung by pictures yet more costly. Giorgione the gorgeous, Titian the golden, Rubens the ruddy and pulpy (the Pan of Painting), some of Murillo's beautiful shepherdesses who smile on you out of darkness like a star, a few score first-class Leonardos, and fifty of the masterpieces of the patron of Julius and Leo, the Imperial genius of Urbino, covered the walls of the little chamber. Divans of carved amber covered with ermine went round the room, and in the midst was a fountain, pattering and babbling with jets of double-distilled otto of roses.[17]

The "otto of roses" may clinch our sense that the narrator frequents barbershops, and dreams such dreams as only dandies under hot cloths dream. Lord Codlingsby, introduced into such splendor, cannot help but be impressed; and he is stunned by the ravishing beauty and culture of Rafael's sister, Miriam de Mendoza. The English aristocrat is no longer listless, but he can only play the ingenu to such wealth and wisdom. Miriam lights his pipe with a thousand-pound note, and as she sings, Rafael draws an instrument from his pocket and accompanies her "in the most ravishing manner, on a little gold and jewelled harp, of the kind peculiar to his nation."[18]

To what degree this parody is anti-Semitic is hard to determine. It does employ the music hall stereotypes of hooked noses, greasy red hair, greed for money—and jews' harps —which the narrator contrives to explain away, or turn into a further advantage of this mysterious and oriental race. But the emphasis of Thackeray's criticism is not on such "realities," for they are brought in only to be transformed by the author's chauvinism and thus function simply as a measure of it. Thackeray seems to limit his concern to this personal quality, and to a few other equally idiosyncratic ones, as we have seen: the narrator's truckling to the aristocracy, the vulgarity of his notions of splendor and beauty (about which he prides himself), and a penchant for absurd political and historical theories, all presented as though from the inside. These personal qualities of course could be fitted to anti-Semitic stereotypes too, but they do not seem to function that way within the parody.

We have seen part of Codlingsby's initiation—the metaphor

of penetration to deeper mysteries is constant—but nothing has prepared him for the final revelation. A strange old visitor turns out to be a king, traveling incognito, who has come to the Duke Rafael for the inside political news of several countries; and as Codlingsby politely leaves, Rafael completes the initiation: " 'Au revoir, dear Codlingsby. His Majesty is one of *us,*' he whispered at the door; 'so is the Pope of Rome; so is . . .'—a whisper concealed the rest."[19] Surely only Queen Victoria could complete the sequence.

Thackeray has done nothing directly with Disraeli's political theory, the vision of an "organically" united England which his recent novels had spent so much of their space presenting. It is a case in which an unsympathetic critic of Thackeray would accuse him of not rising to the really difficult critical job, of avoiding the necessity for thought. But he may just as easily be exercising the novelist's eye for significant detail, in this case, of the human qualities of perception and prose that would doom any idea, however good.[20]

The parody of James Fenimore Cooper shows the narrator standing on the stilts of his stilted prose in order to condescend as an American to all other countries. He shares with most of the other parodied authors a romantic bloodthirstiness that is dressed out as valor. Cooper, for instance, "finds himself forced to adopt the sterner tone of the historian" to describe one of "his country's triumphs," the capture of an English ship by an American:

> Even when the American boarders had made their lodgement on the *Dettingen's* binnacle, it is possible that the battle would still have gone against us. The British were still seven to one; their carronades, loaded with marine-spikes, swept the gun-deck, of which we had possession, and decimated our little force; when a rifle-ball from the shrouds of the *Repudiator* shot Captain Mumford under the star of the Guelphic

Order which he wore, and the Americans, with a shout, rushed up the companion to the quarter-deck, upon the astonished foe. Pike and cutlass did the rest of the bloody work. . . . Peace be to the souls of the brave! The combat was honourable alike to the victor and the vanquished; and it never can be said that an American warrior depreciated a gallant foe. The bitterness of defeat was enough to the haughty islanders who had to suffer.[21]

The brutal side of "valor" also appears in the parodies of G. P. R. James and Charles Lever, and Thackeray is impressive in showing this thread in three such different fabrics. The parody of Lever is entitled "Phil Fogarty, A Tale of the Fighting Onety-Oneth, by Harry Rolliker." Lever had used the pen name "Harry Lorrequer," but "Rolliker" catches more nicely the peculiar "Irish" humor of the narrator and his exploits. When Phil and his gallant friends are pinned down by cannon-fire, their friend the Doctor says, "Who's going to dance? . . . the ball's begun. Ha! there goes poor Jack Delamere's head off! The ball chose a soft one, anyhow. Come here, Tim, till I mend your leg. Your wife need only knit half as many stockings next year, Doolan, my boy . . ."[22]

To the two main elements of excitements and "Irish wit," the narrator must quickly add a third, a little sentiment: "In this way, with eight-four pounders roaring over us like hail, the undaunted little Doctor pursued his jokes and his duty. That he had a feeling heart, all who served with him knew, and none more so than Philip Fogarty, the humble writer of this tale of war."[23]

If Lever celebrates brutality because it is lovably Irish, G. P. R. James rather earnestly respects it, along with money and power. Like Scott, and to some extent Cooper, James seemed to Thackeray to be writing what a recent student of Scott has called "the romance of property," which is marked by a heartfelt loyalty to the status quo.[24] Here is Thackeray's description of the Baron Barbazure (read "Bluebeard"):

> That the Baron levied toll upon the river and mail upon the shore; that he now and then ransomed a burgher, plundered a neighbor, or drew the fangs of a Jew . . .—these were points for which the country knew and respected the stout Baron. . . . Thus lived the Baron Raoul, the pride of the country in which he dwelt, an ornament to the Court, the Church, and his neighbors.
>
> But in the midst of all his power and splendor there was a domestic grief which deeply afflicted the princely Barbazure. His lovely ladies died one after another. . . . So true it is, that if fortune is a parasite, grief is a republican, and visits the hall of the great and wealthy as it does the humbler tenements of the poor.[25]

To underline the point, Thackeray inserts a domestic drama of the sort he was soon to make so much of, in which a girl, in this case Fatima, is rather easily persuaded by her mother to break her lover's vows. Fatima's knight is off on the Crusades and is penniless; therefore she marries Baron Barbazure. The narrator is beside himself with approval of her actions and pretensions:

> Ah! how beautiful and pure a being! how regardless of self! how true to duty! how obedient to parental command! is that earthly angel, a well-bred woman of genteel family! Instead of indulging in splenetic refusals or vain regrets for her absent lover, the exemplary Fatima at once signified to her excellent parents her willingness to obey their orders; though she had sorrows (and she declared them to be tremendous), the admirable being disguised them so well, that none knew they oppressed her.[26]

The remaining parody, "Crinoline," transposes this respect for the social order into modern terms, in the effusions of a Mrs. Gore over the world of fashion, money, and birth.

Altogether, these parodies show Thackeray sure of where he does not stand, through his sensitivity to the connections between popular romances and social order; but equally important, they show him masterfully aware of how a whole standpoint or perspective operates in literature. This ability depends on two main elements: the author's ear for the narrator's voice and his eye for the kind of event appropriate to that narrator. These two aspects join in various ways, as we have seen, but one kind of conjunction deserves more careful attention.

In the narrator's typical description of a sequence of events lies one of the keys to his special view of the world. A crude example of such a descriptive sequence, which Thackeray evidently loved as quintessentially romantic, is the series of impossibly active infinitives followed by the phrase "was the work of an instant." Indeed, he used it so often that by the Cooper parody he could gain comic bathos by *not* ending the sequence that way: "To surprise the Martello Tower and take the feeble garrison thereunder, was the work of Tom Coxswain and a few of his blue-jackets."[27] Aside from being a cliché, what seems to have struck him was the complexity of the series of actions, absurdly telescoped by the last clause into a claim of superhuman address. That such a claim should be made at all, much less in such a routine way, points up at least the carelessness, if not the naïveté or fraudulence, of the narration. In the Gore parody, he experiments with the active-infinitive formula by including touches of slapstick "realism": "To jump from behind, to bound after the rocking, reeling curricle, to jump into it aided by the long stick which he carried and used as a leaping pole, and to seize the reins out of the hands of the miserable Borodino, who shrieked piteously as the dauntless valet leapt on his toes and into his seat, was the work of an instant."[28] But this formula is of course too general to be much more than a symptom of the parodist's interest in the ways things happen and the ways they are described in a given kind of fiction.

Pace—the speed with which the narration proceeds—has something to do with how the narrator looks at himself and his material. In the Bulwer and James parodies, Thackeray points to their inordinate length for nearly opposite reasons: Bulwer's length because he is so busy posturing, and James' because his slow-witted naïveté seems to require very thorough treatment of the most obvious elements—a thoroughness which, as we have seen, does not prevent him from misunderstanding his own materials.

But when at his best in these parodies, Thackeray manages to capture something quite subtle by means of sequences, something more specifically typical of the writer. The second chapter of the Disraeli parody, for instance, is a flashback, a relatively large block of material designed to explain how in the world such an exalted figure as Lord Codlingsby ever met one Rafael Mendoza, and why they should be on such good terms. The joke, however, is that every point in the explanation is a further mystery, and that, for Disraeli, behind the remotest cause is a kind of silence, or rather a whispering we cannot overhear. Mendoza had appeared at Cambridge one day, while Codlingsby was a student, to watch the boat races. That would be clear enough, except that Mendoza watched the races from a little boat which he kept *ahead* of the race. To explain that feat is not, for Disraeli, the work of an instant. For two marvelous paragraphs, Thackeray pursues the explanation in Disraeli's knowing way, while mystery is added to mystery. The boat is so fast because it is "a caïque from Tophana," "the workmanship of Togrul-Beg," who had refused great sums for "that little marvel. When his head was taken off, the Father of Believers presented the boat to Rafael Mendoza."

It was Rafael Mendoza that saved the Turkish monarchy after the battle of Nezeeb. By sending three millions of piastres to the Seraskier; by bribing Colonel de St. Cornichon, the French envoy in the camp of the victorious Ibrahim, the march of the Egyptian army was stopped—the menaced empire of the Ottomans was saved from ruin; the Marchioness of Stokepogis, our Ambassador's lady, appeared in a suite of diamonds which outblazed even the Romanoff jewels, and Rafael Mendoza obtained the little caïque. He never traveled without it. It was scarcely heavier than an arm-chair. Baroni, the courier, had carried it down to the Cam that morning, and Rafael had seen the singular sport which we have mentioned.[29]

The last two sentences are the final flourish of the magician's cape, bringing us back to a world of events we can follow and believe in, while he plays innocent of ever having left it. These are simply the ways things happen, he seems to say, and Thackeray would only add: in Disraelian romance.

Chapter Two

DEVELOPMENTS FROM PARODY

YELLOWPLUSH AND OTHERS

When we turn to Thackeray's output in the ten years between "The Professor" and these parodies, we find him preparing the certainty with which he attacked his narrators and their world views. A large number of Thackeray's early writings owe a good part of their interest to the narrators he invented for them. Charles James Harrington Fitzroy Yellowplush; Isaac Solomons, Jr.; George Savage Fitzboodle, Esq.; Michael Angelo Titmarsh; Major Goliah O'Grady Gahagan—these are only the most important in a long list of fictitious narrators invented in this period. Modern readers are apt to be tempted by the notion that because our attention is thus directed to the way a story is told, Thackeray is exploiting a simple but efficient way of uniting method and meaning: much of the meaning must necessarily inhere in the method.

But there are dangers in looking at the matter this way, for we are apt to ascribe motives to Thackeray which he probably either would not have understood or taken very seriously. Moreover, if we use this notion of union to praise him, we are forced to use it to criticize him, for some of these "unions" are rather awkward and sometimes initial interest in the narrator all but disappears in the course of the story.

There were certainly professional reasons for a writer in 1840, who was trying to support a family and become established, to invent narrators. There was a going market for such inventions, by no means glutted, which had its sources in the eighteenth century—*The Spectator,* Fielding, Sterne, for examples—and it was a market that promised to continue if not increase. We have seen Lever's "Harry Lorrequer," and could quickly swell the list with Dickens' "Boz," *Fraser's* own "Nol Yorke," and so forth. Not only an efficient means of building up a following, and thereby establishing a fund of credit on which a new appearance could draw, the creation of an obviously fictitious narrator had become a minor game in itself that appealed to a taste for "characters," or "originals," and that was primarily associated with comedy. But a full History of Narrators in this period would have to include the dramatic monologues that Tennyson and Browning were writing; Carlyle's Diogenes Teufelsdrock; and, in the more simply comic field, a work by Robert Southey, *The Doctor,* which was running in *Fraser's* when Thackeray began appearing in it. In its remorseless crankiness and violent obliquity, *The Doctor* struck many readers as being indebted to Sterne, but the comparison was not usually to Southey's advantage. J. G. Lockhart, for instance, said that Sterne's materials were "poured out dramatically" through the characters, whereas Southey had "taken the office of showman openly into his own hands."[1] The interest, that is to say, is very nearly limited to the narrator and to the pyrotechnics he will next fire off.

Thackeray's experiments with narrators never went so far. Quick on his verbal feet though he was, and interested in manners throughout his career, he seems to have had from the start a distrust of the merely mannered. He may also have been aware, and distrustful, of what Carlyle called "mere mobility," the hardening of language and emotion into a rigid mode of "improvisation." The term "mobility" seems to go back to Mme. de Staël's *Corrine,* where Byron probably found it,[2] but a full history of the term would lead far afield, especially as Thackeray never seems to have intellectualized such questions. In this case, the path of "awareness"—not to say "influence" —would probably lead back through Carlyle's own practice and his discussions of Jean-Paul Richter to the eighteenth-century English humorists such as Fielding and Goldsmith whom Thackeray already loved and from whom Jean-Paul drew many of his own theories and devices.

If Thackeray knew of the still avant-garde German discussions of wit and humor, or of what became known as romantic irony, either firsthand or as they filtered through the English versions of Coleridge, Hazlitt, De Quincey, and Carlyle, much of what was said would probably have seemed familiar to him from his own experience of the English eighteenth century and even of his beloved Horace. And these reinforcing elements would probably tend to influence him in the direction of the "solid" and "sensible," away from the more frenetic modern discussions and experiments. With his anti-intellectual bent, the problems of distinguishing between Sterne and Jean-Paul, for example, would probably not have struck him as terribly serious ones. Fielding, we can imagine him saying simply, was better than either.[3]

If we look ahead to *The English Humourists,* a series of lectures on eighteenth-century authors published in 1852, the possibility of his lack of interest in mere theorizing approaches certainty. To be sure, he had by then hardened some of his earlier and more flexible positions, perhaps under the pressure of his success as a man of letters; at least he was writing a defense of the guild of "humourists," as well as a pleasant and still interesting introduction to eighteenth-century life and manners. But for whatever reasons, the emphasis throughout is on the character of the author being described, as conveyed through both style and biographical anecdote. Thackeray *likes* Sir Richard Steele, for all his weaknesses, admires the lofty and good-humored serenity of Joseph Addison, thinks Jonathan Swift got out of life pretty much what that broken eagle deserved. As for Sterne, the inventor of new flexibilities in narration—no.

> He fatigues me with his perpetual disquiet and his uneasy appeals to my risible or sentimental faculties. He is always looking in my face, watching his effect, uncertain whether I think him an impostor or not; posture-making, coaxing, and imploring me. . . . The humour of Swift and Rabelais, whom he pretended to succeed, poured from them as naturally as song does from a bird; they lose no manly dignity with it, but laugh their hearty great laugh out of their broad chests as nature bade them. But this man—who can make you laugh, who can make you cry too—never lets his reader alone, or will permit his audience repose: when you are quiet, he fancies he must rouse you, and turns over head and heels, or sidles up and whispers a nasty story. The man is a great jester, not a great humourist. He goes to work systematically and of cold blood; paints his face, puts on his ruff and motley clothes, and lays down his carpet and tumbles on it.[4]

In the earlier years, Thackeray had probably not yet arrived at such certainties, if indeed he ever did, because *The English Humourists* seems as a work so highly influenced by rhetorical considerations about the nature of the original occasion (fashionable lecture halls), of the audience, and of the speaker. He was not repudiating *Vanity Fair,* with all its "motley clothes" and agile, though quiet, highjinks; but he was insisting, in a new and somewhat simplified way, on the difference between "great humourists" and "jesters." We shall examine such changes later in this study, as they appear in the fiction itself. Still, whatever its simplifications, *The English Humourists* should warn us, in our consideration of these early narrators, against looking for any consciously held aesthetic position. It is much more likely that he was simply exploring the possibilities provided by a rather casually accepted and loosely defined convention. Primarily, we find Thackeray's aesthetic delight in the existence of roles, in the comic fact of there being footmen with footman-like ways of looking at the world, or gentlemen like Fitzboodle who distrust all writers but are willing to make an exception of *Fraser's* "Nol Yorke": "I met you once at Blackwall, I think it was," he writes, "and really did not remark anything offensive in your accent or appearance."[5] This is the delight to be found in narrowness, in the genuine article—a delight available, as we saw in the discussion of "The Professor," only to the mind broad enough to enjoy the narrow.

But perfect coherence might grow dull, and Thackeray avoids that danger by means of another and complementary interest. If we think of the footman view, or the gentleman view, as a single set of characteristics, we soon notice that Thackeray is never content with one such set at a time. Always there are several working at once, in a wonderful variety of interrelations. Moreover, the relations among sets not only make variety possible, but are occasionally a positive source of interest as well. The very names of the narrators are formed by opposition, often between heroically pretentious given names and bathetically reductive surnames: Michael Angelo Titmarsh, George Savage Fitzboodle. But it is inwardly, or psychologically, that these relations are able to be explored, if we can so dignify what begins as simply a comic objectification of types.

The earliest example is a Major Gahagan, Major Goliah O'Grady Gahagan, who relates his own "Tremendous Adventures" (1838). He is—and therefore the story is—a collection of simply coexistent sets of characteristics, primarily four: he is Irish and therefore a braggart and liar; but he also has enough pretensions to gentlemanliness to require a transparently thin veneer of modesty; he is an Indian bore, an old military hand whose esoteric jargon conjures up visions of captive audiences yawning over the after-dinner wine; and he is a reader of adventure romances, unconsciously parodying their sham sentiment and real bloodthirstiness in a series of towering tall tales. He exists, then, simply in order to objectify these modes of character. The main "point" of such a story lies in the narrator's ability to say, after describing a father refusing him his daughter's hand in marriage and the father's goodnatured invitation to stay and smoke a pipe with him anyway: "I took one: it was the bitterest chillum I ever smoked in my life."[6]

When "Major Gahagan" began to appear in *New Monthly Magazine, The Yellowplush Papers* was already running in *Fraser's*. The Yellowplush series was a more ambitious work, partly because the sets of characteristics, instead of simply coexisting, are in a state of tension. Thackeray not only is exploring these tensions in themselves, but is using them for social and moral commentary. Stylistically, the voice of Yellowplush, the narrator, consists of rather formal, eighteenth-century syntax; an enormous collection of elegant clichés only occasionally deflated by below-stairs slang; and continual misspelling, which points phonetically in the several directions toward the lower-class pronunciations he still carries with him, toward an imitation of the overheard pronunciations of his "betters," and occasionally toward his total ignorance of the meaning of phrases he has tried to memorize:

Praps he was my father—though on this subjict I can't speak suttinly, for my ma wrapped up my buth in a mystry. I may be illygitmit, I may have been changed at nuss; but I've always had genlmnly tastes through life, and have no doubt that I come of a genlmnly origum.[7]

We took her to Birch's, we provided her with a hackney coach and every lucksury, and carried her home to Islington.[8]

The first story of the Yellowplush series, the lightest, depends on a topical joke something like those cartoons that showed beggars being delivered to their street-corner territories in chauffeur-driven Cadillacs. Thackeray expands this into a pleasant little social analysis, with undertones that the later stories develop. The narrator's employer, Mr. Frederic Altamont, Esq., takes rooms in a shabby genteel household. Because his name and manner are so high, there is more than a suggestion that he is an aristocratic seducer, bearing down on the innocent Cinderella in this household of wicked stepsisters. But he is really in love with her, marries her, and carries her off to the modern equivalent of a castle; and the tension among Yellowplush, his employer, and the girl's house, which between them they had bracketed, seems resolved: "If ever a young kipple in the middlin classes began life with a chance of happiness, it was Mr. and Mrs. Frederic Altamont. Their house at Cannon Row, Islington, was as comfortable as house could be. Carpited from top to to; pore's rates small; furnitur elygant; and three deomestix: of which I, in course, was one."[9]

But there is a mystery about Frederic Altamont, Esq., for not even Yellowplush knows what he does every day between ten and six. His wife's fears and suspicions, fed by the first of Thackeray's terrible mothers-in-law, threaten this state of social and marital bliss. The story ends with a series of reversals which comment on that state, as well as on the narrator: Altamont is discovered to be a crossing sweeper but love survives this breakdown of the social order and, worth six thousand pounds, he is a very well-to-do crossing sweeper, able to live abroad with his wife. He is not, however, able to retain the snobbish Yellowplush. "Of cors, *I* left his servis. I met him, few years after, at Badden-Badden, where he and Mrs. A. were much respectid and pass for pipple of propaty."[10]

By this point, passing for people of property is only the last in a series of confusions and interchanges of illusion and reality. Who, after all, *is* Frederic Altamont? The fairy tale basis of the story seems to indicate that the lovers belong squarely in the center of reality, surrounded by the illusions of Altamont's servant and mother-in-law, and his disguise as a shuffling old crossing sweeper. But the money he earned is real, his upper-middle-class manners are real, he really has to leave England, and he now passes as a land-supported gentleman. To put it another way, the joke is primarily on Yellowplush and his assumptions. But these assumptions are not simply illusions: the polar tension between Yellowplush and the story he has told is unresolved, and adds to the comedy.

In the second story of the series, the tension of the first is deepened and complicated, as though Thackeray were struck by the possibilities in his narrator's remark, "Of cors, *I* left his servis." Yellowplush is now working for the Honorable Algernon Deuceace, youngest son of Lord Crabs. Deuceace is a swindler, or at least could be described so if he were not a gentleman. "It's only rank and buth that can warrant such singularities as my master show'd."[11] We become aware of three moralities operating simultaneously: the insolent criminality of Deuceace, contemptuously cheating an innocent middle-class young man; the self-seeking and amoral "honor" of Yellowplush, concerned for his "suvvant's purquizzits" and the technical loyalty of servant to master; and somewhere off in a spiritual limbo, held by no one but present throughout the story, a more conventional morality which condemns the first two. The first two moralities are held together by Yellowplush's snobbishness, his pride in working for the fifth son of an earl, as well as by the victim's own eagerness to be flattered by an earl's son. What gives the story its strange quality is the ease with which Yellowplush injects the perfectly irrelevant third morality: "Master said nothink, but he *grin'd*—my eye, how he did grin. Not the fowl find himself could snear more satannickly."[12] Or again: "If you could but have seen the look of triumph in Deuceace's wicked black eyes, when he read the noat! I never see a deamin yet, but I can phansy 1, a holding a writhing soal on his pitchfrock, and smilin like Deuceace."[13]

This reaction is not quite hypocrisy, which may be why it is so unsettling. Yellowplush is using two moralities: one is real for him, and the other luridly overstated and unreal. But as there is a kind of devilish malignity about Deuceace, the overstatement of the narrator's language captures something very weird, not to say evil, in the morality of "rank and buth" to which Yellowplush primarily subscribes.

The last and longest of these stories allows Thackeray room to examine this situation from various aspects, but its main elements have all been sketched. Yellowplush and Deuceace are abroad, where with his recent winnings Deuceace is pretending to be the wealthy son of a Lord.

With his glass in his i, he staired at everybody. He took always the place before the fire. . . . I've always found through life, that if you wish to be respected by English people, you must be insalent to them, especially if you are a sprig of nobilaty. We *like* being insulted by noblemen,—it shows they're familiar with us. . . . While my master was hectoring in the parlor, at Balong, pretious airs I gave myself in the kitching, I can tell you; and the consequints was, that we were better served, and moar liked, than many pipple *with twice our merit*.[14]

The dowagers, of course, are after Deuceace to marry their daughters, as they would be "if Sattn himself were a lord." But if this is critical of the established morality, there is a further turn of the screw when Deuceace, on the trail of an heiress, takes to churchgoing: "He made his appearans reglar at church . . . and you'd have thought . . . as he berried his head in his nicely brushed hat, before service began, that such a pious, proper, morl, young nobleman was not to be found in the whole of the peeridge. It was a comfort to look at him."[15] Yellowplush means mainly that it was a comfort to the dowagers watching this show, for they wanted to believe in the coexistence of nobility, piety, and virtue. But in the possibility that it was also a comfort to Yellowplush lies the strain of social insanity that we noticed in the last story, and that finally is seen to underlie the dowagers' willingness to be comforted.

In fact, one sort of insanity—a frenzy of selfishness fed by social conditions—comes very close to the surface in the story of Deuceace's downfall. This characteristic is present in the theme of "Hell hath no fury like a woman scorned" (crucial but never stated) in the story of a cold-hearted young widow who, having been rejected by Deuceace, first entices him into fighting a duel in which he loses a hand, and then cleverly maneuvers him into a marriage with her ugly and penniless stepdaughter. It is present, too, in our final glimpse of him: "He was drest in a shabby blew coat, with white seems and copper buttons; a torn hat was on his head, and great quantaties of matted hair and whiskers disfiggared his countnints. He was not shaved, and as pale as stone."[16] When his victors, the widow and her new husband, notice him and drive off, laughing "peal upon peal, whooping and screaching enough to frighten the evening silents," "DEUCEACE turned round. I see his face now—the face of a devvle of hell! Fust, he lookt towards the carridge, and pinted to it with his maimed arm; then he raised the other, *and struck the woman by his side*. She fell, screaming."[17]

But primarily—at least most originally—the insanity is visible in Deuceace's father, Earl of Crabs, who is the young widow's new husband. In his good-humored, lecherous treachery, he is a villain born of Thackeray's interest in the tensions and distances between moralities. It is the humor Crabs finds in pretending to virtue which is most impressive. He has, for example, a little set piece on tobacco: " 'A bad habit, Algernon; a bad habit,' said my Lord, lighting another seagar; 'a disgusting and filthy practice, which you, my dear child, will do well to avoid. It is at best, dear Algernon, but a nasty idle pastime, unfitting a man as well for mental exertion as for respectable society; sacrificing, at once, the vigour of the intellect and the graces of the person.' "[18]

Against a father who delights so in the very act of hypocrisy, the relatively direct viciousness of his son is helpless. At one point, when Deuceace has written his father a transparently false letter, full of protestations of familial affection, Crabs replies:

> We were all charmed with your warm remembrances of us, not having seen you for seven years. We cannot but be pleased at the family affection which, in spite of time and absence, still clings so fondly to home. It is a sad selfish world, and very few who have entered it can afford to keep those fresh feelings which you have, my dear son.
>
> May you long retain them, is a fond father's earnest prayer. Be sure, dear Algernon, that they will be through life your greatest comfort, as well as your best worldly ally; consoling you in misfortune, cheering you in depression, aiding and inspiring you to exertion and success.[19]

There is in Crabs a strong element of the traditional figure, out of sentimental comedy and gothic romance, of the roué: all natural passions spent after a life of license, and impelled to occasional and mischievous action only by greed and lechery, those unnatural passions. Thackeray was soon to use such a figure in *Catherine* (1839). What distinguishes Crabs, however, is his intellectuality and exuberant self-mockery, the half-suppressed giggle of delight in playing so preposterous a role as that of the "fond father."

Next to the narrator, and in many ways parallel to him, Crabs is the most important thematic character in the story. He helps to show that this society at its most successful can only produce roués, at its least successful human castoffs like his ruined son, Deuceace. Crabs also helps us to see the moral position from which Thackeray is regarding society. His literary pedigree points to the morality of sentimental comedy, in terms of which inheritance of wealth *ought* to go hand in hand with the discovery of long-lost sons and beloved heirs. But there is also another element which Thackeray has added to that morality and which derives from his interest in moral codes. Social insanity is not only a fury of selfishness but is also a schizoid division into seperate modes of thought. In the hands of a Crabs, Thackeray has discovered, parody can be used to present the tensions between these modes, tensions which Crabs himself is aware of and finds funny.

Yellowplush, as we have seen, also presents this division and is conscious enough to record it. He is Crabs' spiritual servant, and the relation becomes actual when Crabs bribes him not to warn Deuceace of his impending doom and at the same time buys his professional loyalties.

The Yellowplush Papers enables us to see Thackeray as a man of his time who was essentially middle class and conservative, and who found as a young writer the imaginary Eden for his nostalgia reinforced by traditional and public literary conventions. But we should also notice where his artistic and intellectual energies are being spent. The relations between these energies and a writer's "character"—or between such expenditures and what seem to him at the time unquestionable truths—are a proper subject for the literary biographer. But the critic finds himself forced, by his very choice of emphasis, to wonder which is more important: the lost Eden of unity between piety, wealth, and virtue ("It was a comfort to look at him"); or the analysis of the breakdown of that unity? The story is about breakdown and one might leave it at that. Still, many readers feel that the central truth about Thackeray is to be found in his unexamined nostalgia, and this argument is not simply the result of careless and reductive reading.

I would argue that, for the writer, the exploration of parody does not lead directly to an examination of basic positions. The grounds of parody are always "true," and function simply as that which makes parody possible. What we have been examining in Thackeray is an exploration out through parody to the character of the narrator, and the further step to making the narrator himself display the state of society. And because this last stage is not static, but seems to point toward the eventual analysis of the assumptions from which parody began, we have a figure of development something like a circle, or spiral—although Thackeray's circle has not yet, at this point, come round.

CATHERINE AND SHABBY GENTILITY

The differences between circles and life, however, may prepare us for a number of detours, among them Thackeray's two crime novels, *Catherine* (1839) and *Barry Lyndon* (1844). Although only the second is told by the kind of narrator we have been considering, both share an interest that is clearly related to and can be seen to develop out of the impetus behind the creation of Yellowplush or even Gahagan. In both novels, Thackeray turned his attention to public modes of thought, and evidently set himself the task of doing something about them in a way more direct than the simple exposure of Yellowplush.

In *Catherine,* Thackeray's target is a particular kind of fiction, which is sometimes called "Newgate" because it often took actual stories of crimes from *The Newgate Calendar* and which treated the stories fictionally in ways that Thackeray found deplorable. The stories and their treatment, he saw, constituted a whole mode of fiction whose differences in examples were less important than their similarities. The later parody of Bulwer, "George de Barnwell," which we have considered, offers a special case of the genre but includes its essential characteristics: wide-eyed thrill in vicarious crime and sentimental confusion of values. The fact that the "Newgate" novel was not a subliterary mode, like our own *True Confessions* or the Mickey Spillane and Ian Fleming stories, but included the work of some of the most respected writers of the period, may give some weight to *Catherine.* The impression of thinness remains, however. The story itself is a simple sequence of betrayals among scoundrels, most of whom are hanged in the end. It is relieved occasionally by a portrait like that of the young rake seen in his forties, already mentioned, who is now a burned out and foolish old man, all but incapable of desire.

To tell the story, Thackeray invents Isaac (Ikey) Solomons, Jr., whose Jewishness is supposed to indicate the economic motives behind the Newgate fiction. Because Solomons is convinced of the worthlessness of the story, Thackeray uses his interjections to condescend to both the story and the reader's supposed taste for that sort of thing; but Solomons' comments generally remain interjections, too separate from the story in both method and content to be very interesting. Their content is separate because the apparent issue, which Solomons ironically describes as that between "dull virtue, humdrum sentiment" and "agreeable vice," simply names by inversion a subject that remains largely unexplored in the book. For the first time in his career, Thackeray's interest in modes has led him into a crude and heavy irony.

> About the year One Thousand seven hundred and five, that is, in the glorious reign of Queen Anne, there existed certain characters, and befell a series of adventures, which, since they are strictly in accordance with the present fashionable style and taste; since they have been already partly described in the "Newgate Calendar"; since they are (as shall be seen anon) agreeably low, delightfully disgusting, and at the same time eminently pleasing and pathetic, may properly be set down here.[20]

Yet despite the difficulties with narration, and the fact that the book derives so much of its meaning from other books, *Catherine* still has a certain mild energy which is the direct result of its announced intentions. In undertaking to show that there is nothing particularly mysterious and therefore titillating in betrayals and murders, no interesting cosmic uncertainties hovering in the neighborhood of crime, Thackeray must show that it is vice, not virtue, that is "humdrum"—not boring, to be sure, but explicable as the result of very simple mechanisms. The real truth about murderers, Thackeray seems to be saying, is the ordinary savagery of their ordinary emotional states. Murder occurs between people who fear and hate and despise each other, for very ordinary and unpleasant reasons. It is here that the book develops most of its power.

Catherine hates her husband and decides to murder him because of the reappearance of Count Galgenstein, her early seducer and the father of her son. That the Count is now a brainless wreck of a man escapes her; with her husband out of the way, she thinks the Count will marry her and provide for their son, a worthless bully whom the Count actually despises. She will be turning the clock back to her youth, be rid of that miserly coward, her husband, and become a Countess, all at once. The Count, naturally, has no intention of marrying her, but is bent on seducing her again, and he thinks he can safely offer marriage. Such elements, together with the catalytic mischief-making of an aged swindler named Wood, are nearly all that this butchery requires. Not mystery, but intense, ordinary, unpleasant frustration is at the center of this world:

> The woman looked at him [Hayes, her husband], thought what she might be but for him, and scorned and loathed him with a feeling that almost amounted to insanity. What nights she lay awake, weeping, and cursing herself and him! His humility and beseeching looks only made him more despicable and hateful to her.
>
> If Hayes did not hate the mother, however, he hated the boy—hated and feared him dreadfully. He would have poisoned him if he had had the courage; but he dared not: he dared not even look at him as he sat there, the master of the house, in insolent triumph. O God! how the lad's brutal laughter rung in Hayes's ears; and how the stare of his fierce bold black eyes pursued him! Of a truth, if Mr. Wood loved mischief, as he did, honestly and purely for mischief's sake, he had enough here. There was mean malice, and fierce scorn, and black revenge, and sinful desire, boiling up in the hearts of these wretched people, enough to content Mr. Wood's great master [the devil] himself.[21]

Frustration "that almost amounted to insanity"—very much like the frenzy to which we saw *The Yellowplush Papers* progress—motivates here a set of characters who, far from being glamourously energetic and interestingly clever, are "wretched." Q.E.D., and the source of much of the novella's power.

Catherine proved that murder could be "shabby"; "A Shabby

Genteel Story" (1840), an up-to-date version of "Cinderella," proves that fairy tales can be shabby when translated into the marginally middle-class world that Thackeray was beginning to invent. Not only that, but the world of shabby gentility contains mute inglorious Cinderellas—real ones. Part of the pleasure of the story lies in its ringing changes on the fairy-tale story itself and part in its filling out of the fairy tale, setting it in a boardinghouse at Margate, a rather seedy watering place, in the off season.

The Cinderella, Caroline Gann, is given brutal stepsisters, all right, but it is her own mother who is cruel, and the stranger who falls in love with her, comparing her to Cinderella, is a foolish artist whom she ignores. Another stranger, also a boarder, seems to her like Prince Charming, but is not: he begins paying attention to her, for instance, only to vex the slightly lurid sisters who have resisted his seductive wiles. Like those of Catherine's aging Count, Prince Charming's desires increase as Caroline resists, until in a mock ceremony he marries her and carries her off. On that unpromising note the story ends, though it was to be continued twenty years later in *The Adventures of Philip*.

So much of the later Thackeray is in this early novelette that one can see why he chose to continue it. The narration is usually at ease, in full command of a world of flyspecked detail and grim or good-humored pretensions. That this was a new kind of parody for Thackeray, drawing not on a contemporary writer's work but on the conceptual framework provided by "Cinderella," seems to have given him the assurance to take possession of this world. It is as though bringing the story up to date gave warrant to the seedy details, ensured their interest, and thereby freed their inventor to imagine more of them. Cinderella's father, for instance, has suffered reverses. He was the good-natured heir to a firm grown rich providing oil for London streetlights, but then came *gas,* his downfall, the move to Margate, taking in boarders, and a pretense at activity:

> On the wire window-blind of the parlour was written, in large characters, the word OFFICE; and here it was that Gann's services came into play. He was very much changed, poor fellow! and humbled; and from two cards that hung outside the blind, I am led to believe that he did not disdain to be agent to the "London and Jamaica Ginger-Beer Company," and also for a certain preparation called "Gaster's Infants' Farinacio, or Mothers' Invigorating Substitute,"—a damp, black, mouldy half-pound packet of which stood in permanence at one end of the "office" mantelpiece; while a fly-blown ginger-beer bottle occupied the other extremity. Nothing else indicated that this ground-floor chamber was an office, except a huge black inkstand, in which stood a stumpy pen, richly crusted with ink at the nib, and to all appearance for many months enjoying a sinecure.[22]

But even such a reversal of fortune can be reversed: Mr. Gann was actually much happier in his "misfortune." He had never liked work, and he much preferred the gin and beer to which he was "reduced," to the wine he had to drink as a wealthy gentleman. "His tastes were low; he loved public-house jokes and company; and now being fallen, was voted at 'The Bag of Nails' and the 'Magpie' before mentioned, a tip-top and real gentleman, whereas he had been considered an ordinary vulgar man by his fashionable associates at Putney."[23]

There is no room in the Cinderella story for a father; why not, however, give her an ineffectual one, whose poverty will make plausible her kitchen drudgery, especially if he is living on his wife's small income and ill-tempered sufferance? He might even, within the limits of his function, prefer gin to wine: the possibilities of invention must have seemed endless.

Once located, the newly discovered country of "A Shabby Genteel Story" was to become relatively independent of the

Cinderella pattern which had served as its formal "constitution." From *The Yellowplush Papers,* Thackeray brought to his shabby genteel world the *ingenuity* of chicanery, persecution, and betrayal with which that series culminated. Crime might still be shabby, but in "Men's Wives," a series of three stories published in 1843, it was not only domestic—scaled down from outright murder—but above all clever.

In the longest of the three stories, "The Ravenswing," there is a distant memory of Cinderella in the story of a vain, coquettish, but good-natured girl, Georgianna Crump, sought after by both a tailor and a barber but finally carried away by a gentleman charmer—who turns out, alas, to be a swindling promoter. Her silly devotion to him makes his calm exploitation of her, and his plausible condescension to her, seem all the more clever. The story culminates in the account of an intricate newspaper campaign to prepare England for her singing career, and his wily use of that very preparation to free himself from debtor's prison. The ending of the story prefigures the end of *Vanity Fair,* in marrying the widowed Georgianna to her faithful and generous tailor, but the story's triumph lies in its successful introduction of ingenious chicanery into the world of Berkeley Square. It is a noticeably unsentimental story: Georgianna owes most of her success as a singer to the politics of publicity and a pair of eyes "as black as billiard balls," and nearly as big; when her manager-husband sets up a mistress in St. John's Wood on her income, she perhaps retaliates with lovers, although we cannot be sure. Luckily, he dies of alcoholism, and she is free to leave the theater and marry her loyal protector, the tailor. Still, the tone is largely comic, and most of the ingenuity is good-humoredly reported. The tone darkens in the other two stories of the series, "Mr. and Mrs. Frank Berry" and "Dennis Haggarty's Wife."

In the first, Frank Berry is shown as a boy bravely battling the school bully, and then, years later, as a husband increasingly helpless against the more subtle bullying of his bluestocking wife. At a momentary check to her growing power, she "gave a martyrized look, and left the room; and while we partook of the very unnecessary repast, was good enough to sing some hymn-tunes to an exceedingly slow movement in the next room, intimating that, though suffering, she found her consolations in religion."[24] In "Dennis Haggarty's Wife," the tone becomes positively grim, the ingenuity practiced on poor Dennis Haggarty, an Irish surgeon, almost grisly. The girl he loves spurns him because of her pretensions to wealth and higher class; but after smallpox destroys her looks and sight, she marries him, accepts his devoted nursing of her for a number of years, takes his money and finally, with the help of her mother, drives him from his house. What strikes the narrator most is the absence of hypocrisy in all their ingenuity, an infuriating dullness that protects the mother-in-law and daughter from any suspicion of their own claims to virtue:

> His troubles are very likely over by this time. The two fools who caused his misery will never read this history of him: *they* never read godless stories in magazines; and I wish, honest reader, that you and I went to church as much as they do. These people are not wicked *because* of their religious observances, but *in spite* of them. They are too dull to understand humility, too blind to see a tender and simple heart under a rough ungainly bosom. They are sure that all their conduct towards my poor friend here has been perfectly righteous, and that they have given proofs of the most Christian virtue. Haggarty's wife is considered by her friends as a martyr to a savage husband, and her mother is the angel that has come to rescue her. All they did was to cheat and desert him. And safe in that wonderful self-complacency with which the fools of this earth are endowed, they have not a single pang of

conscience for their villainy towards him, and consider their heartlessness as a proof and consequence of their spotless piety and virtue.[25]

Together with the ingenuity of persecution in the shabby genteel world, Thackeray had discovered another great subject to be explored and a major extension from parody: "that wonderful self-complacency with which the fools of this earth are endowed." Ingenuity and self-complacency were the subjects of his first novel, *Barry Lyndon,* published the year after "Men's Wives," and the shabby genteel world was temporarily abandoned for the world of an eighteenth-century adventurer.

BARRY LYNDON AND *THE BOOK OF SNOBS*

Catherine had begun as an answer to Newgate fiction and was weakened by its dependence on that external "problem"; *Barry Lyndon* faces its own problems in the creation of a character who tells his own story. When it first ran in *Fraser's,* a certain amount of narrative apparatus accompanied it, in the device of an editor collecting Lyndon's papers and occasionally commenting on them. This device made the work seem simpler than it is, made it seem a fairly straightforward case of unwitting self-exposure on the part of a criminal whose editor, at least, was not at all taken in. But when it was republished, in 1856, Thackeray cut most of the editorial apparatus, and the book emerges more clearly and powerfully, independent of Newgate fiction and the need to insist on the criminality of crime, and independent even of its great predecessor, Fielding's *Jonathan Wild.*

Fielding had explored a witty conceit: Jonathan Wild was a great man, as he so often insisted, because his crimes exactly paralleled the crimes of those whom the world agrees to call great. Without the constant parallelism, there would be no "greatness." Thackeray's Lyndon, however, half-believes in his family's royal heritage, and in any case will fight the man who doubts it. From the start, therefore, his claims to "greatness" are a good deal more complicated than Wild's. Having erected Lineage into a private principle, however willfully, he is then free to fight—and often win—battles in an actual society that is rigidly class conscious. Fielding's parallelism provides fairly straightforward, though richly inventive, irony; Thackeray's method, which might be called triangulation, provides a much richer mixture, and introduces an element of victimization of this Irish blackleg adventurer beneath all his later self-justification. Compared with Jonathan Wild, Barry Lyndon is much more fundamentally identified with the society on which he preys, he objectifies it and turns it back on itself. It is within this framing relationship that the book's variations and progressions occur—and within it, too, that questions of the author's or reader's identification with this antihero need to be discussed. Because Lyndon's self-exposure is the exposure of society, he becomes a scapegoat, as well as a villain, and it is primarily the strain of pathos rising from his being victimized that saves the book from being merely "pure irony."

In the first of three sections, Lyndon, who begins life as Redmond Barry, the poor relation of a reduced Irish family, fights his way from grammar school through his first love-duel and escapes to the Continent, to be caught up in the Seven Years' War and be taught the life of a professional gambler by his uncle. In the second section, he returns to England and Ireland, pursues and marries the Countess of Lyndon, heiress to the largest fortune in England. The third section recounts his triumph and downfall, when he lives for a time in Fleet Prison, tended by his fierce old mother "as a baby almost, [who] would cry if deprived of his necessary glass of brandy."[26]

With the sections, the amount and type of self-exposure

varies, so that it becomes a kind of principle of development. Indeed, there is almost too abrupt a change in the type of self-exposure between the second and third sections, though it is not, finally, arbitrary.

The narrator records his boyhood and youth with an avuncular fondness and pride, noting the spirited delusions of his earlier self—his beloved was actually a vulgar and rather homely flirt, the duel was a put-up job arranged with blank cartridges—and noting aside from the fierceness, a good-humor worthy of Defoe's Moll Flanders, or Cleland's Fanny Hill. For both the fierceness and the untroubled good-humor, the scapegrace energy, there is a fond though somewhat condescending pride. Self-exposure is largely in the keeping of the narrator himself, except for an occasional interruption of another character's scorn for his lack of principle, as when a messmate in a European army calls his clever betrayals spying. The threat of violence, however, accepted as the proper defense of honor, quiets such occasional interruptions.

In the second section, self-exposure is hardly the word for the management of the narrative. Lyndon is in perfect alignment with the world of Bath and Dublin, its utter and appropriate master. The problem, as everyone there sees it, is to marry the Countess of Lyndon, a silly bluestocking surrounded by sycophants and married to the dying Sir Charles Lyndon, who married her for her money. Barry Lyndon marries her after a campaign of inventive ingenuity that is one of Thackeray's most impressive inspirations. Immune to the insults of the enviously moralistic, and of the cynical Sir Charles himself, and welcoming the Countess' scorn as a sign of interest, Barry "surrounds" her: Does she like windy discussions of transubstantiation and flowery Arcadian eloquence? He can buy theological arguments for a crown, and easily speaks the language of flowers. Does she feel supported in her exalted station by family, other lovers, law, society? He can buy servants, scare off her defenders using their own standards of physical courage, and overawe her superstitious mind by proofs of the extent of his powers, carefully arranged.

He is hardly one of those to whom "nothing is sacred"; in fact it is precisely the pieties of this culture in which he is most learned and adept. True, the pieties of rank, birth, money, and social cohesiveness are not particularly mysterious to him yet, as truly functioning pieties are. But that is why there is no self-exposure, in the ordinary sense, in this section. What could be hidden, he might ask, that would require exposure? Pieties, he seems to say, are simply matters of power, so the ingenious student of pieties need never be at a loss for power.

In the third section, self-exposure accompanies self-justification: as he runs through the Countess' fortune, it is scoundrelly tradesmen with rascally bills, confounded influence peddlers who do not provide what they have been paid for, and devilish bad runs of luck at cards that do him in. It is a curious hodgepodge of complaints and failures that accompany the record of his downfall, leading us to look for some principle of coherence in this version of the old story of the biter bit, the rascal outrascalled.

Whatever the principle is, it is hardly the eventual triumph of justice, and not even the notion of Lyndon's overreaching, although he is certainly guilty of that. In the main, his downfall seems to come because his world is now too mysteriously complex, in all its varied matter-of-factness, to be controlled by him. Other people want the Countess' money, too, and will employ legal power to get it. In part, then, he is now the target for the same sorts of trickery he once practiced, is on the defensive and surrounded; but a quasi-spiritual change has taken place in him. Its signs are that almost nothing "works": he cannot even win at his old profession, gambling. It is as though, in winning the Countess and her fortune, some connection between the world and himself has been cut. It is a curious effect, underlying all the self-justification that provides the self-exposure of the third section.

The source of this internal change is indicated in the first sentence of the third section: "All the journey down to Hackton Castle, the largest and most ancient of our ancestral seats in Devonshire, was performed with the slow and sober state becoming people of the first quality of the realm."[27] That word "becoming" is a crucial one. In what sense does Barry Lyndon take pleasure in the solemn progress to Hackton Castle? And what does he mean by "*our* ancestral seats"? Any questions are soon resolved. He quickly begins to take seriously, in the third section, the values he had so ingeniously manipulated in the second. He even loses a great deal of money trying to buy a title for himself and his son. There is still plenty of the old rapacity left in him, but the good-humor that had accompanied it and had been based on his own lack of pieties is gone, hardened into social attitudes (like his Toryism) "becoming" to his new station. He falls victim to "that wonderful self-complacency with which the fools of this earth are endowed," and because the self-complacency is composed of social attitudes, he is in part a scapegoat.

With *The Book of Snobs,* which was running in *Punch* as *Vanity Fair* began to appear, Thackeray's early concerns join in a somewhat uneasy mixture. Casual as the book is in format (a collection of sketches, more or less extended, of various kinds of Snobbishness), Thackeray had found his first really large subject, and the difficulty with the book is that he needed the larger ground of the novel to explore it.

The definition of Snobbishness is deliberately elusive, partly because the narrator enjoys toying with the earnest conventions of social analysis, and partly because the subject proliferates in several directions. As the examples of Snobbishness pile up, the reader is forced to try increasingly general definitions, perhaps the best of which is a negative one: "With love and simplicity and natural kindness Snobbishness is perpetually at war."[28] But even that is too subjective in its formulation. Snobbishness is that which prevents life from occurring, is the enemy of spontaneity and freshness, as in the example of the British Snob abroad: "Art, Nature pass, and there is no dot of admiration in his stupid eyes: nothing moves him, except when a very great man comes his way . . ."[29]

As the book moves toward generalization, it becomes clear that Thackeray is talking about something extremely broad and conceptually fertile. His concern is with the private language each person uses to think about himself, and it is really this ineradicable necessity that causes all the trouble. But because the terms of each character's "language" are in part derived from society, we are confronted by a whole civilization comprised of villainous scapegoats, like so many milder Barry Lyndons. "Honesty," and the other activities of the spirit with which "Snobbishness is perpetually at war," would be of some use. But the force of the narrator's announcements that he, too, is a Snob derives from the attained sense that Snobbishness is a kind of psychological synonym for Original Sin.

Writing to Robert Bell about Fielding's *Tom Jones,* a year later, Thackeray denies any distinction between Fielding's hero and his villain. "You have all of you taken my misanthropy to task—I wish I could myself; but take the world by a certain standard (you know what I mean) and who dares talk of having any virtue at all? For instance Forster says: After a scene with

Blifil, the air is cleared by a laugh of Tom Jones—Why Tom Jones in my holding is as big a rogue as Blifil. Before God he is—I mean the man is selfish according to his nature as Blifil according to his."[30] But he is talking mainly about, and trying to defend, *Vanity Fair*.

Chapter Three

VANITY FAIR: POSTURES OF WISDOM

THE "ETHICAL" ARGUMENT

The style of every writer constructs some relation to his audience—indeed it "constructs" that audience in an important sense—and, as readers of *Vanity Fair* know, Thackeray is more than usually explicit about the narrator's relation to his story and his audience. After considering his earlier work, we can understand his concern with narrators, but to many modern readers this aspect of the novel is simply irritating. One has called it the steady drip of pronouncement. Henry James thought it spoiled the illusion of history, on which the future of the novel form depended. Yet, if we step outside the conventions of storytelling to which we have become accustomed, Thackeray's manipulation of the storyteller's intrusions is interesting in itself and fulfills several perfectly valid artistic functions, as well as being relevant to larger aspects of his novel.

To begin with the narrator is to find the welter of Thackeray's style reduced, and at least provisionally organized. There on the surface, in apparent conflict, are two different conventions jostling each other, one now uppermost and now the other:

one I shall call, temporarily, "satire"; and one, "realism." These are modes of thought, as much as of expression, which Thackeray seems to delight in manipulating into sudden juxtapositions. It is as though, temporarily at least, there are two different "brotherhoods" being addressed: one, the audience of satire; and the other, that of realism. But these terms need some explanation. Whether or not his work purports to be "A Novel without a Hero," as *Vanity Fair* does, a satiric narrator might of course be his own comic hero. Given a place to stand, he might implicitly promise to pry up, lift into notice and isolation for the purposes of criticism, the particular world which is his subject. Speaking of Becky and Sir Pitt, the narrator of *Vanity Fair* says, "Such people there are living and flourishing in the world—Faithless, Hopeless, Charityless; let us have at them, dear friends, with might and main. Some there are, and very successful too, mere quacks and fools: and it was to combat and expose such as those, no doubt, that Laughter was made."[1] In this statement are most of the standard elements of satire: the narrator's confidential relations with his audience; his "place to stand"—in this case, apparently, an assumed and easily granted Christianity; and his confidence in the face of the enemy. Despite his exhortation to "have at them," the satirist's audience evidently need only look on as he outwits and outparries their mutual enemies, and winks at his audience over his shoulder.

Realism is of course a more difficult concept to define, particularly because its formulations in English and American literature have never hesitated to include ethical norms. It claims to be no less moral than satire, but where satire normally assumes in advance the values by which its subject is to be judged (that is, refers outside the work to certain values), realism claims to discover its value within its subject, in operation, as it were. Typically, a work claiming to be realistic contains built-in modes of unreality, which function as opposing alternatives to the truth. Even the unvarnished tale needs some sort of varnish to contradict.

It was evidently Thackeray's decision, in a book that includes an almost endless variety of contradictions, to use satire as one of the contradictions of realism. Because the satirist can caricature his victims, Thackeray constructs the whole puppeteering rigamarole, the steady series of announcements that this is just a story, that there are "some terrific chapters coming."[2] But the realist quickly turns "chapter" into a metaphor: "Are there not little chapters in everybody's life that seem to be nothing, and yet affect all the rest of the history?" For the realist, his pocket full of such surprises, this is a nonliterary, unvarnished record of Life, of which "every word is true," and in which are discovered the author (equipped with an imaginary wife named Julia) and even "the reader" mingling among the characters. Tom Eaves, a gentleman-about-town who knows everything, was one source of the story; and the narrator met Dobbin abroad with Amelia and young George. You and I—or rather our formal surrogates—turn up also, in comments and asides that are central to the realist's purpose: "We say (and with perfect truth) I wish I had Miss MacWhirter's signature to a cheque for five thousand pounds. She wouldn't miss it, says your wife. She is my aunt, say you, in an easy careless way, when your friend asks if Miss MacWhirter is any relative. Your wife is perpetually sending her little testimonies of affection, your little girls work endless worsted baskets, cushions, and footstools for her."[3] The result of this sort of shift in focus is, of course, a very much larger Vanity Fair. To the satirist—and to John Bunyan—Vanity Fair is a separate domain, walled and recognizable, on the spiritual landscape. To the realist, however, the walls are down, and citizenship in that city has become universal. All men are in Vanity Fair instead of the other way around—instead of Vanity Fair being merely one of many spiritual possibilities.

Three working beliefs help remove the boundaries. The first is the idea, taken simply as a truth of experience, that the bad are seldom so bad, or the good so good, as simpler moralists—here, the satirists primarily—would make out. Second is the expanded list of qualifications for citizenship. Any unworthy motive will do and, failing that, as in Dobbin's case, any unworthy object of desire. And third is an interest in the effect of social environment on morals, which tends to support the first belief:

> If people would but leave children to themselves; if teachers would cease to bully them; if parents would not insist upon directing their thoughts, and dominating their feelings—those feelings and thoughts which are a mystery to all (for how much do you and I know of each other, of our children, of our fathers, of our neighbour, and how far more beautiful and sacred are the thoughts of the poor lad or girl whom you govern likely to be, than those of the dull and world-corrupted person who rules him?)—if, I say, parents and masters would leave their children alone a little more,—small harm would accrue, although a less quantity of *as in praesenti* might be acquired.[4]

I shall want to use this example for other reasons, but for now it may serve to indicate how pervasive, inescapable, and even ineradicable Thackeray considers the stain of worldliness to be. The self-confidence of satire is clearly inappropriate to such a world, even though some of the values of the satire may still be necessary for understanding this world. Satire alone is "unrealistic."

The relations between the two modes of satire and realism, then, are various. On the surface they are simply juxtaposed, and their friction produces a kind of fireworks of sparks. But more important, the opposition between satire and realism reinforces the realism's claim to reality; and in addition, the moral force of the satire is deflected onto the areas assumed to be real. That is, by undermining the insulated self-sufficiency of the satirist's position, realism triumphs over satire, as it were, by proving itself more inclusive and trustworthy. And on the other hand, the values that the satirist holds and that enable him to satirize are not really replaced by a different set of values, but are simply assimilated into the larger position.

It was evidently part of Thackeray's rhetorical design to combine the two modes into the voice of a citizen preacher. That is, in the midst of the sermon, at the end of a particularly interesting *exemplum,* he could gain a preacher's best effects by turning to the smug congregation with a knowing "And you?" or a confessional "And I?" The citizen preacher is a kind of synthesis, the resolution for the conflict of opposing modes, who "realistically" insists on the universal relevance of his criticism. And just as the satirist has been submerged in the figure of the lay preacher, the satirist's audience, seen now as a brotherhood of the *fortunately* good, has joined the crowd around the jester's platform and must serve as his targets. One function of Thackeray's style, therefore, is to *dramatize* and objectify the traditional "ethical argument"—that is, the construction of a group and of the speaker's right to address it.

The anticlimax at the end of the passage about children just quoted serves as a kind of verbal equivalent of the cap and bells in which Thackeray dressed this creature for his frontispiece, a position constructed in part by sly buffoonery. If only, begins the earnest realist, such and such were the case, if only we would do this or that—whereupon the sly buffoon breaks in with the last word, "small harm would accrue."

That example of his style is typical in other ways. Until the shift in tone that deflates its earnestness, the sentence is built on a formal pattern of sound (the sonorous expansion of an "if-then" construction) that is periodic in its anticipation of a thundering close. Its formality is qualified, though not lost track of, by the interrupting parenthesis. The difficulty for Thackeray, even with such mild figures of sound, is that they convey not only formality but also the very sound of moral earnestness, and are therefore closely akin to the cant he so distrusts and so often parodies. And the difficulty is increased by the high incidence of abstract diction that points at moral profundities—"beautiful" and "sacred," for instance—and points at them also by way of character types such as poor lads and girls, world-corrupted persons.

Much of Thackeray's style seems to have been formed during the years he worked on *Fraser's,* and this final shift to buffoonery may simply remind us of what Miriam Thrall calls that magazine's "violent protest against ostentatious or elaborate style and overstressed sentimentality or emotion."[5] Yet Thackeray has gone beyond *Fraser's* in dramatizing stylistically that rebellion and, at the same time, using both sides of the conflict. I have already mentioned how the second part—the anticlimactic increase of distance—deflates the pomposity of the first role, thereby demonstrating the speaker's submergence in Vanity Fair and his right to address its inhabitants. Yet that earnestness was, in the surrounding narration, a real outburst, corresponding to the narrator's impatience with his own urbanity, as though he were letting down his guard for a moment. There is, in other words, no real deflation because the force of the outburst is meant to survive. It is a dramatic form of an explicit statement that he makes later: "O brother wearers of motley! Are there not moments when one grows sick of grinning and tumbling, and the jingling of cap and bells?"[6]

That first example may remind us, too, of how little of Thackeray's wit is epigrammatic, as well as how rarely he uses explicit metaphor. We come to expect parody, the assumption of an indentifiable and ludicrous role, and irony, the manipulation of distance between statement and meaning, which seems a natural extension of his concern with the kinds of distance I have been describing. This is evidently a style elaborately suited to a preoccupation with roles and with the attitudes they embody.

As is usual in literature, then, the ethical argument—the construction of a group and of the speaker's right to address it—turns out to be part of a much larger concern. Concentrating on the narrator's relation to his audience, we have found Thackeray extremely conscious of it, using roles felt to be inadequate to reflect on each other and thereby to indicate a more adequate one.

The point is a simple one, perhaps, and I have dwelt on it at such length partly in order to work out and put to use an assumption that seems to me crucial for an understanding of Thackeray. That is, in avoiding any talk of effectiveness or persuasiveness, I have assumed that the only audience we can discuss at this point is the audience seen as a reflexive function of particular modes of address and thought. "Realism" and "satire," as I have described them, in one of their dimensions "define"—call into existence—a particular audience, and would do so if no one ever enjoyed the book at all.[7] It is Thackeray's working awareness of this fact that allows him to write as he does.

But this concern would be too limited unless one could show its relevance to the larger issues of the novel. The connection is provided stylistically, it would seem, by the more general phenomena of shifting tones and distances.

THE AWARD OF SYMPATHY

The following passage may seem at first to have nothing to do with roles, certainly nothing apparent to do with the narrator's relation to his audience; and it may seem like nothing so much as one of those children's jokes to which we are supposed to respond, "That's good; that's bad." Yet it will probably strike most readers as being typical of narration in *Vanity Fair*.

> By the side of many tall and bouncing young ladies in the establishment [Miss Pinkerton's], Rebecca Sharp looked like a child. But she had the dismal precocity of poverty. Many a dun had she talked to, and turned away from her father's door; many a tradesman had she coaxed and wheedled into good-humour, and into the granting of one meal more. She sate commonly with her father, who was very proud of her wit, and heard the talk of many of his wild companions—often but ill-suited for a girl to hear. But she had never been a girl, she said; she had been a woman since she was eight years old. Oh, why did Miss Pinkerton let such a dangerous bird into her cage?
>
> The fact is, the old lady believed Rebecca to be the meekest creature in the world, so admirably, on the occasions when her father brought her to Chiswick, used Rebecca to perform the part of the *ingénue;* and only a year before the arrangement by which Rebecca had been admitted into her house, and when Rebecca was sixteen years old, Miss Pinkerton majestically, and with a little speech, made her a present of a doll—which was, by the way, the confiscated property of Miss Swindle, discovered surreptitiously nursing it in school-hours. How the father and daughter laughed as they trudged home together after the evening party (it was on the occasion of the speeches, when all the professors were invited), and how Miss Pinkerton would have raged had she seen the caricature of herself which the little mimic, Rebecca, managed to make out of her doll. Becky used to go through dialogues with it; it formed the delight of Newman Street, Gerrard Street, and the Artists' quarter: and the young painters, when they came to take

their gin-and-water with their lazy, dissolute, clever, jovial senior, used regularly to ask Rebecca if Miss Pinkerton was at home: she was as well known to them, poor soul! as Mr. Lawrence or President West. Once Rebecca had the honour to pass a few days at Chiswick; after which she brought back Jemima [Miss Pinkerton's sister], and erected another doll as Miss Jemmy: for though that honest creature had made and given her jelly and cake enough for three children, and a seven-shilling piece at parting, the girl's sense of ridicule was far stronger than her gratitude, and she sacrificed Miss Jemmy quite as pitilessly as her sister.[8]

Some readers have the same kind of trouble with passages like this in *Vanity Fair* that they have with *Moby Dick*. Although I would not push the analogy very far, there is, just beneath the urbane surface, a kind of bewilderment that may be fully as baffling as Melville's love of mystery.

Logically, the subject of the sequence is Becky, who is seen among rapidly shifting contexts: childhood, poverty embattled and poverty dissolute, female purity, Miss Pinkerton's cage. Yet not only the contexts but the attitudes toward these contexts change. And then there is that doll, which serves as another point of intersection, more objective, of different contexts. The doll is Becky's reward for playing so well—so exaggeratedly—the role of ingénue. She is given it at sixteen, eight years after becoming a woman. It is the occasion for a ludicrously majestic speech by Miss Pinkerton, headmistress of this snobbish boarding school, who did not buy but confiscated it from a little girl caught nursing it in class—a little girl whose father's name, alas, is Swindle. In Becky's hands, the doll becomes the agency of a caricature and justice; then the toast of dissolute bohemians; and, finally, as though it had introduced a spirit of pitiless caricature, a companion at the sacrifice of Jemima, Miss Pinkerton's kind and well-meaning sister.

The difficulty for the reader is that there are apparently no logical links between, no hierarchy among, these contexts. Each item seems to embody a firm attitude, but it has no obvious relation to the next item. Poverty, dissoluteness, dunning, and swindling all seem to be equally bad. Female purity and innocence, good humor, and justice seem good. Cleverness is evidently neutral ground.

Admiring critics of Thackeray have usually cherished this kind of sequence as proof of his maturity. In such narration, they feel, Thackeray gives us the sense of life's complexities, of the interpenetration of good and bad. But whereas we can agree with these critics that the point of the passage is not simply disapproval, not a pox on all these houses—Sharp's, Pinkerton's, Swindle's, society's—we are apt to be struck by a certain lack of complexity here, a mere juxtaposition of houses. Thackeray's air of criticism, of constantly shifting evaluations, turns out to be in one sense illusory. It is pseudo criticism, as I. A. Richards might say. Yet the passage is not therefore empty. Its point, its "argument," is primarily stylistic. The passage is pseudo criticism in the positive sense, because it gives the feeling of being evaluative; and it achieves this effect by exploiting the rhetorical possibilities of shifting distances and perspectives. What is left, after all rational grounds for judgment have cancelled out one another, is the abstract feeling of judging itself, the play between more and less sympathy. For all his air of genial urbanity, the narrator seems to be surrounded by a disparate and bewildering group of people, events, situations, whose only possible claim on him is sympathy. Not justice or morality, but sympathy is in question here, as it is most explicitly in the sacrifice of Miss Jemima when, despite her kindness to Becky, she is pitilessly mimicked. Had Thackeray wanted to continue this sequence, we may speculate, he could have emphasized Miss Jemima's foolishness—here, she is simply "that honest creature." He ends the sequence with what was its common denominator, stylistically and to a minimal extent logically, the question of sympathy. Duns, Miss Pinkerton, Swindlers, callous bohemians, and finally Becky herself, carried away by her triumph, we finally see do share something: they are not sympathetic.

To the extent that the narrator shifts distance, by awarding or withholding sympathy, and shifts contexts, he is shifting roles, and in a way that is much more basic to the book than the relatively superficial construction of the ethical argument. Yet because sympathy alone is the common property of the sequence, the importance of the roles here is simply that they shift. None of them casts any light on the others or can really be seen as the resolution of any others. To sympathize with Sympathy might seem a sufficiently objective center were it not so abstract as to be almost completely formal; and, like "falling in love with Love," which it somewhat resembles, it is primarily self-reflexive.

Another way of putting the matter is that the light shed is primarily reflexive, illuminating the mind of the observer in the act of responding. The "world" of this narration is rather firmly dualistic, and our interest in the world is largely limited to seeing it brought under a certain kind of contemplation, a genial and emotional scrutiny. I do not mean that there is nothing "out there" for the narrator, nothing beyond his own mind. In fact the style may testify to a certain amount of anguish over the very "otherness" of the world. But the focus of style—its main interest, as it were—is on the variety of perspectives available to the mind. It projects a kind of psychological relativism.

Near the end of his biography of Thackeray, Gordon Ray discusses something like this question: "Profoundly aware of the 'streamingness of experience' (in Geoffrey Tillotson's phrase) he avoided wherever he could the delusive short-cut of abstraction."[9] Mr. Ray was not talking about short passages but about the total sense of Thackeray's works. Yet in a passage like the one we have examined, the style is not simply antirational, anti-intellectual; it might be called antimonistic: some link, some belief in the mind's ability to make sense of the world, has been cut, or at least greatly attenuated. Superficially, Thackeray seems to resemble the Fielding whom he admired so much; but Fielding would have been incapable of writing the passage we have examined, for somewhere in such a passage, however complex, the sly and genial position of Good Sense would have triumphantly emerged.

In themselves, of course, such perspectives need not cancel one another. Indeed the use of multiple perspectives ordinarily implies a periphery, and rather easily suggests a point of intersection for the angles of view: perspectives are ordinarily taken to be perspectives *on* something. In his essay on Cervantes, Leo Spitzer implies that the history of perspectivism after *Don Quixote* may be summed up in the title of Pirandello's play, *Six Characters in Search of an Author*: six perspectives in search of a common center.[10] But Carlyle, for instance, was able to convince a good many of his generation that his perspectives pointed at some Great Ineffable Substance; indeed all the Victorian Sages, as John Holloway calls them, experimented with means of indicating what they thought to be true perception, means that we might often call perspectivist.[11] If Thackeray does not really belong with the rest of his contemporary sages, perhaps the reason will be found not in his perspectivism, but in his curious uses of it.

CHAPTER THREE

PERSPECTIVES AND WISDOM

I have already discussed two structural perspectives, one fairly concrete and one quite abstract: the dramatization of the "ethical argument" and the play of sympathy. Both are created linguistically by juxtaposition: the one, by placing "realism" next to "satire"; the other, by placing more specific attitudes alongside one another. In their different ways, both are examples of what Kenneth Burke calls "perspective by incongruity,"[12] though he might want to save that term for more startling examples. Yet the idea of a created and conscious perspective, in both its general and linguistic senses, probably subsumes the idea of incongruity—at least a mild incongruity seems necessary if only for discrimination. Some information theorists use the word "entropy" to describe the provision for surprise in a communications system. Systems can be classified as being primarily "redundant" or "entropic," depending on how great a possibility for new information is built in. Thackeray's "system," they might say, is highly "entropic," because he is so constantly engaged in juxtaposition. In more literary terms, this habit of juxtaposition helps to explain why the linguistic unit in Thackeray is a sequence: not the word but the anomalous phrase, such as "A Novel without a Hero"; not the sentence but the paragraph or page, as in the two sequences about children and about Becky and her doll that we have already considered.

In the last decade, the work of several critics has helped to isolate many of Thackeray's habitual perspectives. Two critics especially, John A. Lester, Jr. and Geoffrey Tillotson, have considered some of his artistic habits in detail, and have begun to relate those habits to what we are calling "perspectives," modes that project a certain sense of life.[13] Mr. Lester confines himself to narrative techniques, primarily of two kinds: "redoublings," in which the narrator interrupts natural chronology in order to go back in time and work up again to the original stopping point; and a variety of kinds of "semi-scenes," which are midway between direct, dramatic presentation and summary narration.

The redoublings (sixty in *Vanity Fair)* are not to be explained simply by Thackeray's instinct, as a storyteller, to plunge into the middle of things, and the consequent need to fill in background later. Nor can redoublings be explained by the requirement of serialization for climactic endings of parts which would have to be accounted for in the next installment, because, in the unserialized *Henry Esmond,* Mr. Lester counts the greatest number in any of Thackeray's novels. They are rather to be accounted for primarily by "the nature of his material," and by "motives of temperament"—in other words, by the general perspectives that they help to establish, although Mr. Lester does not use the term in this sense. That is, they not only make possible the presentation of certain kinds of material, but present in themselves certain ways of looking at that material. They can show life to be panoramic, and so they are used to present simultaneous and connected actions. Life, too, is largely a matter of human reactions for Thackeray, and as a general rule redoublings abound in the vicinity of a dramatic scene, in order to explore reactions and their causes.

Finally, redoublings are related to Thackeray's handling of time, to his "retrospective vision" of life. This vision is discernible not only in that all his novels are more or less historical and are told from a position in time long after the facts related, but also in the continual shifting of temporal perspectives, even within a scene. At a given point in the story time, for instance, we will hear not only Becky's reaction to events but her memory from years later of those events and reactions. We are often told not only what is happening, but how it will all come out. Redoublings, then, like the "retrospective vision" which they help to construct, present the view of all events spread out at once in a panorama, the view of human virtues and vanities in the "long result of time"; they allow events to be seen "in the light of their consequences," and "characters now in the press of present action, now in the mature and deliberate retrospect of after life."[14]

Some of the principal kinds of "semi-scenes" that Mr. Lester defines are the "habitual," the "intermittent," and the "interjected quotation." The habitual scene is usually introduced by "Clive would say," or "Captain Rawdon often said." The intermittent scene—"a running sequence of scenic glimpses"—may be several pages of brief subscenes interspersed with narrative commentary. Another common kind of semi-scene is the result of quotations injected suddenly into the narrative description of events; these interjections allow the narrator "freedom to reminisce over his narrative at will, yet always be able to call on his characters to speak their own words and confirm the point he is making."[15] Other, less common kinds of semi-scenes are the "purely allegorical," such as Darby and Joan, Jones and Brown; "imagined" scenes, where the narrator "fancies" that it must have been something like this; and even invitations to the reader to compose scenes from his own experience. Indeed, "there is seemingly no end to Thackeray's invention of semi-dramatic scenes."

What these kinds of semi-scenes share, what makes them perspectives, is that they are all in some sense "illustrative":

> They are all offered as being significant because, beyond their artistic value as discriminated occasions, they illustrate a truth of character or human behavior which Thackeray means to convey. It

goes without saying that his allegorical scenes exist primarily to illustrate a general moral truth. It is nearly as obvious that his habitual scenes do the same; they convey enduring, recurrent traits of character rather than momentary or chance reactions under the stress of an actual scene.[16]

What Mr. Lester is describing might be called wisdom perspectives—classical allusion is another—that may or may not be actually wise. To decide that question involves discussing what kind of worldly wisdom Thackeray educes from the world, what kinds of characteristic traits he can imagine, whether or not classical allusion in a particular context is actually wise, and so forth.

These structural perspectives convey part of Thackeray's sense of where truth is to be found and of the appropriate way of looking for it. They construct a kind of morphology of truth. They suggest that life, in order to be understood, *requires* being looked at panoramically, timelessly, retrospectively. These very abstract ways of seeing "pay off" in understanding, the book assures us, a fact it tries to demonstrate internally. As formal properties of the work, these postures of wisdom are necessarily very abstract. They are abstract not because more recent novelists have found any ways to avoid such postures, but because, as sheer postures, they have as yet very little intellectual content. Philosophically, that is, we need to distinguish between postures of wisdom and wisdom itself. Artistically, although we may share Mr. Lester's admiration for Thackeray's inventiveness, we need to discover the sources of tension that bring these formal properties to life.

Perhaps largely from irritation with these allegations of wisdom and truth that spring up in so many discussions of Thackeray (the second volume of Gordon Ray's biography is entitled *The Age of Wisdom*), a fairly large group of critics in the last fifteen years have felt it necessary to even the score by denying or limiting severely these claims for Thackeray's fiction. All these critics have helped to clear the air by calling into question specific meanings that they find presented in Thackeray. Although all of them would thus be relevant to the discussion at this point, Dorothy Van Ghent's chapter on Thackeray in *The English Novel: Form and Function*[17] is most important to our purposes because she seems to be speaking the language of perspectives.

Indeed, one of her charges against Thackeray is that he is guilty of "a clumsy mishandling of perspectives,"[18] by which she means that she feels a strong sense of disparity "between the author's person and his work, his opinions and his creation." Part of her sense of disparity depends on a separation she sees between the life presented in the novel and the narrator's reflections on it. Mr. Tillotson has gone to great lengths to answer effectively such a charge by demonstrating the generally inseparable interpenetration of comment and narration, of "fact" and judgment.

Still, Mrs. Van Ghent might be right in a larger sense in seeing a disparity between two general perspectives, of which she thinks the smaller disparity is only symptomatic. These larger perspectives she calls "compositional centers," and she sees one as "actually functioning" and the other as "weak and unavailing."

> The actually functional compositional center of *Vanity Fair* is that node or intersection of extensive social and spiritual relationships contributed by Becky's activities: her relationships with a multitude of individuals . . . and, through these individuals, her relationships with large and significant blocks of a civilization. . . . But beside this violently whirling and excited center is another, a weak and unavailing epicenter, where Amelia weeps, and suffers and wins—wins Dobbin and solvency and neighborhood prestige and a good middle-class

house with varnished staircases. Organized around the two centers are two plots, which have as little essentially to do with each other as Thackeray's creative imagination had to do with his sentimental, morally fearful reflections. He cannot bear to allow the wonderfully animated vision of Becky's world to speak for itself, for its meaning is too frightening; he must add to it a complementary world—Amelia's—to act as its judge and corrector.[19]

A logician might call the form of Mrs. Van Ghent's argument, "poisoning the well," for much of her description of this antithesis depends on her contempt for its source: Thackeray's alleged fearfulness. But the substance of her argument is harder to deal with. For whatever reasons, there may be two such opposed perspectives on life contradicting each other in *Vanity Fair*. Mrs. Van Ghent shares with most of the other adverse critics of Thackeray a strong sense that much of the life he describes is unbearable, morally sick, a life in which people are, for instance, ferociously cruel to each other. No wonder, then, that for these critics all palliation by Thackeray, in a plot or through commentary, should be a further sympton of disorder. Joseph Sedley, for example, seems to Mrs. Van Ghent "one of the most complicated psychological portraits in the book," in both his personal and socially representative aspects: "We see in Jos's obesity the sickness of a culture, the sickness due to spiritual gourmandism, or, in simpler but still metaphysical words, to overeating; in his shyness of women, the repressions and abnormalities of a sick culture; in his stupidity and febrile conceit, the intellectual numbing and tubercular euphoria of a culture."[20]

Applying an organic theory of art, then, together with the assumed power to identify and analyze the activities of the different mental faculties, Mrs. Van Ghent sees Thackeray's "creative imagination" committed and marvelously fertile in one perspective, one general mode of thought that establishes for her felt connections between Joseph Sedley and Lord Steyne, Becky and the Crawley clan, but that has nothing whatever to do with the "morally immature fantasy"[21] of the Amelia plot. Mr. Tillotson seems to share a very much milder version of the same sense. "Out of his mouth . . . flows the brook of talk, touching all the terrors, but accepting them without knowing very well what else to do about them."[22] And even so admiring a critic is willing to settle for a dichotomy between Thackeray's ideas and his "pictures." In the next chapter we shall try to escape such distinctions by examining some of the working ideas by which those pictures are constructed, especially the main notions Thackeray held about psychology and causation. Perhaps we can escape, too, the insidious infiltration of faculty psychology—the easy assumptions about which parts of the author's mind are at work in different sentences and scenes—by using a method that cuts across such distinctions.

Chapter Four

VANITY FAIR: WISDOM AND ART

THE PATTERN OF WISDOM

In *The Mirror and The Lamp,* M. H. Abrams dealt suggestively with the ways in which terms like those of his title have served historically as emblems for certain large-scale patterns of belief. "Mirror" and "lamp" refer most directly to notions about the nature of the mind (it passively mirrors the world, or it more actively illuminates true reality), but each such notion about the mind is almost necessarily part of a larger pattern of belief that also includes notions about the nature of reality. The handy metaphor, "mirror," then, far from exhausting the meaning of the pattern, indicates a part of it, very dimly suggests the rest, and furthermore limits the pattern to questions of epistemology and ontology, which are regarded as the chief terms of the pattern.[1]

But in many writers, one finds another kind of root metaphor, one that seems to be almost physically derived by the writer, and underlies and shapes much of his thinking whatever his subject matter. We may think of "marriage" in Wordsworth, the yoking together of "affinities," or the intricately interlocking "oneness" of Coleridge. In these cases, there is a strong kinesthetic element in the pattern, the result perhaps of both artistic choice and habitual metaphoric thinking. Such a particular, recurring pattern seems to be one of the ways a mind habitually organizes experience. Of course any mind uses many such ways, but some will probably seem to the individual more "right" than others; particular patterns may easily come to seem the very shape reality ought to take. If so, these characteristic patterns could operate whether the mind is working "creatively" or "reflectively"; but the frequency of a certain pattern might change from the desire for a certain kind of result or in the presence of certain kinds of material. Mr. Abrams was concerned to explore patterns common to an age; we would be looking for patterns in a single writer. In Thackeray's case, I have already mentioned the linguistic habit of juxtaposition, of "perspectives by incongruity," and we have seen Mr. Tillotson find "narrative" everywhere in Thackeray, a sense of "the streamingness of experience."

Applying this approach to Thackeray may seem to be inordinately complicated because he is obviously so interested himself in "forms," "patterns," "roles." Indeed, "roles" may be said to be the subject of *Vanity Fair*: whatever Miss Pinkerton's reasons may have been for introducing Becky into her school, one of Thackeray's reasons was surely to bring up, by means of this "little actress," the subject of roles. But, paradoxically, his interest helps to simplify the problem because "forms" and "roles," as he conceives them, are part of a recurring pattern.

In this pattern, forms are the external expression of an essence. In one sense the pattern is, of course, common to all minds, in any generation; it is a method by which we reduce complexity to its "essentials," and is why the pattern is so useful—and so dangerous. But for Thackeray, the relation between the terms of the pattern is itself questioned: it is as though he carries in mind both the complexity of things and their essence, and he tends to prefer the essence and to distrust the complexity. Perhaps this preference resulted from the pressure of several intellectual forces in his society that tended to treat complexity as the "expression" of the "essence," but separable from it. An essence may have several possible expressions, and once this idea is accepted, there is no question about where value and truth are to be found.

Three main forces in the early nineteenth century, all related to one another, probably have a great deal to do with the prevalence of such a pattern: evangelical Christianity, the domestication of Romanticism, and the attempt to salvage the "essence" of Christianity from the wreck of its dogmatic forms. All these forces meet in the work of a man who wrote for the same magazine during Thackeray's apprenticeship, and whom Thackeray for a long time regarded as one of his heroes, Thomas Carlyle.

Arthur Pendennis, the hero of Thackeray's next novel, uses a concept drawn from Carlyle that depends on this pattern. But the narrator scolds Pendennis because he has used only half the pattern; his awareness of the existence of "forms" in the world is leading toward a dangerous relativism.

> To what [the narrator asks the character] does this scepticism lead? It leads a man to a shameful loneliness and selfishness, so to speak—the more shameful, because it is so good-humoured and conscienceless and serene. Conscience! What is conscience? Why accept remorse? What is public or private faith? Mythuses alike enveloped in enormous tradition. If seeing and acknowledging the lies of the world, Arthur, as see them you can with only too fatal a clearness, you submit to them without any protest farther than a laugh . . . if the fight for truth is taking place and all men of honour are on the ground armed on the one side or the other [except you], you had better have died . . .[2]

Pendennis, the next book after *Vanity Fair,* is more ambitious than its predecessor because Thackeray seems to be consciously trying to deal with issues implicit in *Vanity Fair.* In the passage just cited, Pen is aware of "mythuses"—one of Carlyle's favorite words—but, dazzled by their existence, he fails to try looking "underneath" them for the truth that must be down there, under these "lies." It is not, apparently, clear where the truth is, under there, but Pen and his narrator would both recognize immediately the *force* of Carlyle's argument about the Old Testament—"Hebrew old clothes"—because the pattern is the same. In *Sartor Resartus,* Carlyle moves toward replacing this pattern with a more "organic" one—"natural supernaturalism"—that promises to unite the essence with new forms of expression, new "mythuses." Thackeray evidently does not follow him that far.

Carlyle himself can be seen as an example of "the domestication of Romanticism" as he not only imported some of the ideas of the German Romantics, but tried to find domestic and middle-class applications for them. Thackeray is a domesticator in a simpler sense because he finds "truth and nature" in the bosom, as in the following passage from *Pendennis.* The narrator is describing the late eighteenth-century sentimental drama by von Kotzebue, *The Stranger:*

> Those who know the play of the "Stranger" are aware that the remarks made by the various characters are not valuable in themselves, either for their sound sense, their novelty of observation, or their poetic fancy. . . . The Stranger's talk is a sham, like the book he reads, the hair he wears, and the bank he sits on, and the diamond ring he makes play with—but, in the midst of the balderdash, there runs that reality of love, children, and forgiveness of wrong, which will be listened to wherever it is preached, and sets all the world sympathising.[3]

In general, *Vanity Fair* may be called "The World in Clothes" chapter of Thackeray's *Sartor Resartus,* and *Pendennis* a conscious attempt to say more clearly what "The World Out of Clothes" is like. But these are the two sides of a coin, the halves of a pattern that underlies and is common to at least three large areas of *Vanity Fair:* its psychology, its view of events and causation, and its philosophical dualism.

PSYCHOLOGY

Psychologically, Thackeray's basic concept is that of an emotional "center" within the self which is pure and innocent, and full of loving kindness, and which seeks "expression." In the process of giving expression to this inner essence, however, difficulties occur. Selfishness is the first level of externality, at which the emotional force is reflected back on its source. Hearts become crusted over with selfishness, but they can sometimes be taught to open. To be true and honest, in *Vanity Fair,* is to give expression to the inner self. So far, this cluster of beliefs may sound all too conventional; but Thackeray complicates these conceptions by distrusting all social roles, indeed all externality. Roles do not help to define the self, as they do for many of the earlier Romantics, but simply distort it. Externality is not only the subject, but finally, the villain of the book.

We have already seen one application of this root metaphor in the comment on the mental lives of children and their world-corrupted seniors: ". . . those feelings and thoughts which are a mystery to all (for how much do you and I know of each other, of our children, of our fathers, of our neighbour, and how far more beautiful and sacred are the thoughts of the poor lad or girl whom you govern likely to be, than those of the dull and world-corrupted person who rules him?) . . ."[4]

And speaking of Rawdon Crawley's love for his son, the

narrator says, "The very best and honestest feelings of the man came out in these artless outpourings of paternal feeling . . ."[5] Here is another example: "Which of us . . . can tell how much vanity lurks in our warmest regard for others, and how selfish our love is? Old Osborne did not speculate much upon the mingled nature of his feelings, and how his instinct and selfishness were combating together."[6] Here the "instinct" of paternal love is not only better but deeper and truer than mere selfishness, which is not an "instinct." Thackeray's sense of mixed motivation can usually be interpreted, as it can here, by reference to the root metaphor of an inner emotional self struggling for expression against external frustrations.

This account of the underlying pattern in Thackeray's psychology seems simple and reductive, for much of his talent and attention is directed to "the life of the mind" of a special sort. One of the many meanings of the word "vanity" to Thackeray is, of course, that of the vanity mirror which men hold up to themselves by creating ideas about themselves. They have a positive "hunger of the imagination," in Samuel Johnson's phrase, a fierce mental energy directed toward creating a self-congratulatory gestalt out of the psychic materials available to them. To create and preserve this cocoonlike mode of thought they will commit any crime.

"Openness," then, though it ultimately proceeds from the heart, is most often prevented by these rigid modes, and rigidity of any sort seldom escapes Thackeray's censure. Cant and hypocrisy, his favorite targets, are "formal" vices, for they depend on rigidified codes of language and behavior. One of the "morals" of Henry James, the need to be "large and free and generous," is thus very close to Thackeray's. The range and subtlety of his sensitivities to these modes are wonderful, as every reader soon discovers. Dobbin will be warning George, for instance, of Becky's abilities as an actress, when George is in pursuit of Becky. " 'Humbug—acting? Hang it, she's the nicest little woman in England,' George replied, showing his white teeth, and giving his ambrosial whiskers a twirl."[7]

The causes of the fallen state of human affairs, and specifically the source of this mental appetite, seem not to have concerned Thackeray very deeply. Yet someone so aware of these activities of the mind can hardly be called superficial. One of the main reasons Thackeray did not ask further questions seems to have been the "self-evidence" of the pattern, which accounted for these activities by assigning them a place within it.

CAUSALITY

Another way to locate Thackeray's concern with externality is to notice his special uses of the nineteenth-century novelist's device of playing, within the novel, on the distinction between novels and real life. A primary purpose of this device is to insist on the reality of this particular, unliterary novel. In one typical scene, the bookish heroine arrives at a point when she is unable to read novels any longer. Novels, we are to understand, are ordinarily too pat, whereas her life is both real and complicated. Moreover, the girl is suddenly made aware of her own responsibility for her life: of the necessity for becoming, in at least a limited sense, the author of her own "novel." It is the realistic novelist's counterpart to those scenes in Scott, for example, in which the hero is told, "Now choose, young man!"

But in *Vanity Fair* the device, besides insisting on the reality of the tale, usually carries a very different implication. It also indicates the causes of events: "If he [Jos] had had the courage; if George and Miss Sedley had remained, according to the former's proposal, in the farther room, Joseph Sedley's bachelorhood would have been at an end, and this work would never have been written."[8] Or: "If Rawdon Crawley had been then and there present [at Miss Crawley's], instead of being at the club nervously drinking claret, the pair might have gone down on their knees before the old spinster, avowed all, and been forgiven in a twinkling. But that good chance was denied to the young couple, doubtless in order that this story might be written. . ."[9] Indeed, to consider causation, in this novel which claims to be without a hero, is to be confronted with an almost endless reach of causal factors conceived to be external, and to be acting on one another. Tilted at by a merely satiric narrator and ordered to stop going around, such a windmill world could only reply, "I can't; and what do you mean by 'around'?" Two contrasting series of events may make the problem, and Thackeray's solution to it, clearer. At several points, he seems to have contrasted them consciously: the first sequence of the book, which ends with Jos Sedley not marrying Becky, and a later one, which ends with George Osborne's marriage to Amelia.

In the first sequence Becky's actions, as it turns out, are only one thread in a complex strand of events that she had begun to spin soon after her arrival at Miss Pinkerton's. With the foresight of a chessplayer, she makes friends with Amelia for the sake of Amelia's reported brother, an unmarried Indian nabob. Soon after meeting him, Becky has his proposal "trembling at his lips." Her only problem, apparently, is to "provoke" it. But at this point Thackeray moves in with complications carefully chosen for size and type. Becky's first frustration, due to intricately woven causes, occurs in the drawing room when the teasingly tentative presence of George and Amelia prevents Joseph from proposing. Surely Becky will be more successful the next night at Vauxhall.

Yet she fails again, from an even more complicated chain of facts and events. For her to fail, it is necessary that Joseph, to bolster his courage to propose, should toss off "bumper after bumper of claret" before leaving for Vauxhall. Once there, at a particularly close moment, it is necessary that the bell should ring for fireworks. But chiefly, of course, it is necessary that "everybody had rack punch at Vauxhall" in order for Joseph, showing off, to order some. "That bowl of rack punch was the cause of all this history. And why not a bowl of rack punch as well as any other cause?. . . . Was not a bowl of wine the cause of the demise of Alexander the Great . . .?—so did this bowl of rack punch influence the fates of all the principal characters in this 'Novel without a Hero,' which we are now relating."[10]

Becky's "villainy" is not yet foiled. To be sure, the party leaves before Joseph can propose. But even Joseph's headache and remorse, the delayed effects of the punch, are not sufficient to defeat Becky until George Osborne, the counter-villain, enters as Becky's first conscious opponent. While Joseph is still wallowing in his hangover, George decides to ensure the effect of the punch by so teasing Joseph that the marriage will become impossible. Despite Thackeray's announcement, then, the effects of the punch on Joseph are only raw materials to be shaped and directed by George. "You terrible!" George says. "Why man, you couldn't stand—you made everybody laugh in the Gardens, though you were crying yourself."[11]

Several aspects of this series of events are worth noting. First, the causes divide about evenly between social conventions and Joseph's weaknesses. Both sides combine when George destroys his picture of himself as a gentleman, a picture, or "mode," necessary to his further pursuit of Becky. Indeed, his weaknesses are "social"—what Dorothy Van Ghent means when she sees him as representative of fundamental social disorder.

Second, Thackeray's focus on the bowl of punch, although it is of course a shenanigan of the literary realist, is also—as he points out in the same passage—a matter of concern for the moral realist in "this 'Novel without a Hero' which we are now relating."

Great events stem from relative trivia, we are told, but even the trivia must have antecedents, and are not only causes but themselves effects. Everyone at Vauxhall had rack punch; elsewhere, Napoleon and the princes of Europe must engage in war to further the story. Neither triviality, then, nor mere panoramic sequence is exactly the point. But punch and war do share a villainous look, as well as externality; they have a power to run lives from the outside, and to no good result. Because characters like Becky and George live in externality, they have a kind of blood relation to events. Becky is defeated this time, but she is obviously in her element. Her relation to events is machination, and she and George can accomplish machinations with such ease because they can manipulate the ideas that other characters have of themselves. Thackeray's main notion of causation, then, is deeply appropriate to his psychology. Faced with such a world, what good would a Hero do us?

In the later sequence, which seems to be Thackeray's answer to this question, Dobbin first reveals himself as the unheroic hero of the book: he is unliterary in his heroism because of his big hands and feet, and his lisp; yet, luckily, he is stripped of any idea of himself that Becky could manipulate. George, at this point, is mildly disturbed by the ruin of his fiancée's family, his friends from childhood, and he is touched when his pathetic worshipper releases him from their engagement. The scene is then half-prepared for Dobbin's entry, much as Joseph had been half-prepared for George. In addition, the grounds of the appeal, the activating motive, will be similar for Joseph and

George: their idea of themselves as gentlemen. In Joseph, this idea took a crude form: a gentleman never makes anyone laugh at him, and never cries in public. In George, the concept is more heroic. Among other things, a gentleman is pure in heart and the dashing protector of the innocent. When Dobbin comes to see George, Thackeray explains:

> Dobbin was very soft-hearted. The sight of women and children in pain always used to melt him. The idea of Amelia broken-hearted and lonely, tore that good-natured soul with anguish. And he broke out into an emotion, which anybody who likes may consider unmanly. He swore that Amelia was an angel, to which Osborne said ay with all his heart. . . . And for himself, [George] blushed with remorse and shame, as the remembrance of his own selfishness and indifference contrasted with that perfect purity. . . . "George, she's dying," William Dobbin said,—and could speak no more.[12]

The "perfect purity" that reminds George of his selfishness is evidently Dobbin's as well as Amelia's. Soon after this scene, it works out nicely that George's father, who had brought and paid for George's vision of himself, should try to dissuade him from seeing Amelia and, in doing so, represent to his son all the ungentlemanly forces in the world.

Because of the externality of this idea in George, Dobbin cannot take credit for the outcome. All unconsciously, he simply reminded George of the terms in which George wanted to see himself and the situation. Dobbin cannot take all the credit—must share it with Mr. Osborne, and George's bringing up, and the impending war—though he also cannot take any of the blame that automatically attaches, in this book, to machination. He had simply "broken out into an emotion." His influence may seem slight, but it apparently is Thackeray's most serious alternative to role-playing. He underlines its aspect of unconsciousness: "Without knowing how, Captain

William Dobbin found himself the great promoter, arranger, and manager of the match between George Osborne and Amelia."[13] And of course Thackeray protects Dobbin from all suspicion of selfishness by having him love Amelia by this time. Dobbin's moral triumph here, qualified and hedged though it is, asserts the reality of the pattern I have been describing.

IMPLICATIONS

From Dobbin's triumph to the unqualified bliss of Jane Eyre, whom someone has called a moral steam roller, may seem an enormous distance. Yet in the preface to the second edition of *Jane Eyre,* Charlotte Brontë positively tingled with what Edmund Wilson and Melville have called "the shock of recognition." The distance did not seem so great to her because, I suspect, she simply brushed aside all the complicating differences.

> . . . I think no commentator on [Thackeray's] writings has yet found the comparison that suits him, the terms which rightly characterize his talent. They say he is like Fielding: they talk of his wit, humour, comic powers. . . . His wit is bright, his humour attractive, but both bear the same relation to his serious genius, that the mere lambent sheet-lightning playing under the edge of the summer cloud, does to the electric death spark hid in its womb.[14]

In a much cruder way than *Vanity Fair,* and as though projecting its author's daydreams, *Jane Eyre* makes constant use of a pattern similar to Thackeray's. Jane's surface plainness, for instance, covers "a savage beautiful creature" beneath; many of the scenes and images, like much of the language of prudent "firmness," project repression of energy. Yet Charlotte Brontë's optimism, naïve earnestness, and loyalty to the traditions of romance allow that energy an unqualified final triumph in the book.

Thackeray was embarrassed by Charlotte Brontë's praise, and a visit from her did not go well.[15] He took his humor more seriously than she did, we may say, and it had saved him from imagining the righteous victory of Jane Eyre. Not only humor, however, is involved in the difference. In the sequence we have been considering, several elements might have troubled Jane Eyre. First, the marriage itself is only the best of a bad situation, founded as it is on George and Amelia's illusions about each other. Second, Dobbin's unconscious act has committed him to the performance of a role—that of "the great promoter, arranger, and manager of the match"—and he finds himself, as friend to the new family, often forced into what his author fondly but accurately calls hypocrisy. "Conducted to the ladies ...Dobbin assumed a jovial and rattling manner, which proved that this young officer was becoming a more consummate hypocrite every day of his life. He was trying to hide his own private feelings. . ."[16] And, finally, as Thackeray told Mrs. Liddell, who had begged him to "let" Dobbin marry Amelia: "Well, he shall, and when he has got her, he will not find her worth having."[17]

In fact, there are no objects worthy of desire in *Vanity Fair*. It is as though the root pattern of an inner essence and its distorted expressions has assimilated still another concept—that of the inner emotion and its external object—so that both concepts take the same metaphorical shape. Perhaps the notion of externality made them seem to have a natural kinship. At any rate, these two concepts reinforce each other and together make life seem to a large extent deplorable. Where but in a gentleman's own parlor could he hope to escape Vanity Fair, prove immune to Becky, achieve spontaneous expression? Yet even there, Dobbin discovers, he is not safe: under the hearth is a Victorian abyss. Meanwhile, he is a husband.

Thackeray's modern biographer, Gordon N. Ray, sees the question of inwardness as related to Thackeray's redefinition of the concept of the gentleman. Thackeray, he says, was trying to replace the external view of the true gentleman—a Regency figure measured by the clothes he wore and certain superficial manners—with an emphasis on the proper qualities of mind and heart. This is an aspect of the pattern I have been describing, an application of it; and there is no question but that Thackeray, at the end of the book, approves of Dobbin. But in considering Dobbin's final situation, we are faced with a kind of irreducible dualism. To be sure, externality can only be "seen," be understood, by its opposition to inwardness. But for Thackeray, the two at best can only coexist in a sadly humorous double vision.

As we have seen, the argument of style, the point it makes, is that there is no escape from roles. Just as there is no single language that by itself can indicate the narrator's true role, there is no role that is somehow not a role. Indeed, one may feel that for Thackeray in *Vanity Fair* there is also an abyss under the heart. For the language of the heart is so abstract, so stylized in both speech and gesture, as to suggest that even emotion itself is a kind of role. Perhaps we are only responding to Thackeray's typically Victorian confusion over the nature of emotion, a confusion produced by abstracting emotion from experience. Yet there is a dim, disturbing sense in *Vanity Fair*—stronger than in most Victorian novels and much stronger than in Thackeray's own later novels—that parents and lovers at their best perform roles which are only preferable to other roles. This suggestion is probably what some of Thackeray's contemporaries responded to with the charge of cynicism. We can agree that cynicism is not the point; and, to be sure, Becky does move beyond her author's forgiveness in violating the sanctities of marriage and motherhood by her disloyalty to Rawdon and her cruel indifference to her son. Yet it was perhaps partly to answer the charge of cynicism that Thackeray insisted so strongly in his later novels on these twin sanctities, and made the heroes of his next two novels sadly but gratefully marry motherly girls.

Yet in *Vanity Fair,* Thackeray testifies in several ways to a kind of uneasiness over these sanctified emotions. Not only are the objects of the emotions unworthy, but the emotions themselves are so automatic as to be occasional material for comedy. Mrs. Sedley, for example, was blind to Becky's designs on her son Jos, for the very best of reasons. When her husband warned her of the plot, she was at first determined to send Becky away but changed her mind: "When morning came, the good-natured Mrs. Sedley no longer thought of executing her threats with regard to Miss Sharp; for though nothing is more keen, nor more common, nor more justifiable, than maternal jealousy, yet she could not bring herself to suppose that the little, humble, grateful, gentle governess would dare to look up to such a magnificent personage as the Collector of Boggley Wollah."[18] Both her first reaction and her second, then, turn on emotion which is itself a kind of automatic gesture: maternal jealousy and maternal pride, both too easily called into play.

Similarly, Rawdon Crawley's outburst at discovering Becky with Lord Steyne, which for many readers releases a kind of energy that has been felt to be building up, is so totally in character as to be robbed of much of its significance. His consequent exile and death barely rate a headline.

STYLIZATION AND ART

We may feel that Thackeray has set loose the specter of stylization but cannot entirely control it. It seems to proceed from his very highest talents, but he does not seem entirely sure of what, conceptually, to do with it. All that finally escapes stylization is the unspeakable, the ineffable, indeed the unknowable. I am not thinking of a fairly large class of devices of which this sentence is typical: "Her simple artless behaviour, and modest kindness of demeanour, won all their unsophisticated hearts; all which simplicity and sweetness are quite impossible to describe in print."[19] Her qualities are given expression through the pretense that they are inexpressible. But there is a class of comments that testifies to Thackeray's attempt to set certain areas beyond the reach of any expression. We have already considered two examples: ". . . those feelings and thoughts which are a mystery to all (for how much do you and I know of each other, of our children, of our fathers, of our neighbour) . . ."; and Dobbin's heroic inarticulateness: "'George—she's dying,' William Dobbin said,—and could speak no more."[20]

Chief among these comments are the references to Amelia's prayers. "These, brother, are secrets, and out of the domain of Vanity Fair, in which our story lies."[21] And elsewhere, we hear of her hours of "speechless prayer."[22] To the satirist, prayer would fall outside the domain of Vanity Fair. To the realist, however, the human side of that dialogue, at least, would seem to be an important touchstone in the novel, and one not to be avoided—if, that is, there were a language capable of expressing it. Evidently for Thackeray there is not and Amelia's prayers must remain speechless.

During the composition of *Vanity Fair,* Thackeray wrote to his mother about the book: "What I want is to make a set of people living without God in the world (only that is a cant phrase) . . ."[23] The book, we have seen, claims to do more than that,[24] but in what way "living without God" is a cant phrase to a moralist who still uses the vocabulary of Christianity—"Faithless, Hopeless, Charityless," for example—is difficult to understand. It is only partially explained by G. K. Chesterton's description of Macaulay: "That dropping of the Puritan tenets but retention of the Puritan tone which marked his class and generation."[25]

To insist, as Thackeray more explicitly does in his later novels, that certain preferable roles are reality itself can be seen from one angle as a retreat from the full range of his uneasiness in *Vanity Fair.* It is a very Victorian despair, built as it were on one side of Carlyle and Emerson: like them, he is extraordinarily sensitive to the operations of forms, and he shares, in *Vanity Fair,* their genius for tracing that operation. But whereas they are true perspectivists who are convinced of the intersection of their angles, Thackeray was apparently doomed to suspect that the world out of clothes was a blank. Averting his eyes from that possibility, he falls back on the language of the heart and, when that falters, on an undefined pietism, a Protestantism that protests all forms, including language.

Perhaps, without really explaining the difficulty, we can describe it as the result of a tension between two externally unrelated modes of thought. For the satirist, the root metaphor of the heart and its expressions is a perfectly useful one: it enables him to expose simple hypocrisy, for example, on the assumption that one could simply listen to one's inner being and become honest, if one tried. Those who do not are fair targets for satire. But for Thackeray's realist, and for one as sensitive to the prevalence of forms as Thackeray was, that root metaphor is no longer useful. We might risk the generalization that, for the realist, the world of forms to which Thackeray responded does not afford perspectives on an emotional center within the self, as he sometimes thought it did. The most instinctive response includes formal elements, and so the distinction between emotions and externality falters and necessarily blurs. The figure of the lay preacher, although it was a rhetorical resolution for conflicting modes, is not really a stable enough role, and the platform on which he stands constantly threatens to give way.

Indeed it would be difficult to say what it is that roles, as Thackeray sees them, could have been a perspective on. Some other notion of the self was evidently necessary before he could achieve full intellectual coherence. Certainly he would have had to take the existence of roles seriously in itself and to divorce it from the root metaphor of his satire.

At the least, we cannot join those critics who, like Mrs. Van Ghent, divide *Vanity Fair* into the real Becky half and the unreal Dobbin half. Both halves are equally real and do not so much contradict each other as fail to contradict each other neatly. What was perhaps meant to be an opposition wavers and in this sense Thackeray's uneasiness is fundamental. His occasional optimism and hangdog cheerfulness are compromised and finally undermined by his sensitivity to the question of roles.

We may now see the internal importance of those postures of wisdom I described in the last chapter: "Life is panoramic; truth is timeless; experience streams." When translated from formal, categorical ways of seeing, *postures* of wisdom, into substantive assertions about life in Vanity Fair, each is emotionally ambiguous. To view life panoramically is good because it calls sympathy into play, because it is self-consciously honest and free of illusions, and because the very stance is culturally recommended as wise. But to the sense that true meanings of life are hidden under forms, the panoramic aspect is disturbingly external: neither view is complete by itself, yet neither explains the other.

So it is with all the postures of wisdom. The timelessness of truth versus the "streamingness" of experience; the formal aspects of behavior versus the heart's truth: philosophically and artistically, *Vanity Fair* consists of the tensions between these polar ideas. Unless we read simply for "ideas," they do not function as contradictions but as the sources of a kind of magnetic field in which experience is held in meaningful tension. Other writers, both better and worse than Thackeray, manage to unify experience. Charlotte Brontë, using parts of the same vision Thackeray had, managed to elevate them into an apocalyptic triumph in *Jane Eyre*. Yet few readers out of their teens, and fewer male readers of any age, would prefer *Jane Eyre* to *Vanity Fair*.

The example of *Vanity Fair* may call into question the ease with which many critics and readers, especially since the great Romantics, have equated the function of the artist with the discovery of some kind of philosophical monism, some coherent vision of life. The trouble lies in that word "vision," which is so easily translated into "position." *Vanity Fair* has a vision in the sense that it presents a coherent tension, a pull between mutually reinforcing ways of seeing. *Jane Eyre's* unity, on the other hand, is relatively incoherent because it is produced by a sleight-of-hand manipulation of unrelated "forces"—sex, morality, religion—which, the author pretends, all finally burst into bloom at once and into the same bloom. Because these forces in *Jane Eyre* are not shown to be in any very meaningful relation to one another, the result is that we may well have difficulty experiencing the book; at most we can only wish it were all true. *Vanity Fair* is a nearly opposite case.

Chapter Five

LATER FICTION: CHARACTER AND ACTION

DEVELOPMENT

Of *Pendennis,* the novel after *Vanity Fair,* Thackeray says in his preface that "It fails in art" but "strives to tell the truth." Neither statement seems very helpful now, but both have figured in a disagreement between two of Thackeray's most distinguished modern defenders. *Pendennis* fails in "art"—in the craft that would produce a complex plot moving toward the single denouement of a discrete work of art—because, Geoffrey Tillotson claims, Thackeray's work is all one: to see his true artistic achievement, we must focus not on discrete works but on his total output. Not so, says Gordon Ray. Somewhere in the early 1840's, Thackeray underwent a distinct moral deepening, not to say awakening. For evidence, we have his remarks in letters and in this very preface, in which as a novelist he accepts the challenge to try to tell the truth, presumably in order to make men better.

Mr. Tillotson seems to have the better of the argument when he points out that nothing Thackeray wrote is devoid of moral concern and, presumably, didactic intent, and that the most noticeable increase in earnestness occurs in private and public statements about what he was attempting all along in his art. The increase in such pronouncements probably does, however, indicate his growing self-consciousness as a popular man of letters and, perhaps, his growing self-confidence in that role—unless these statements be interpreted as whistling in the dark, as self-flattery designed to keep up his confidence. I suppose they could reflect both confidence and the hunger for more of it.

But there are real changes in the novels after *Vanity Fair,* both technical and substantive, that do require discussion. Altogether, they do not add up to the record of a large spiritual growth, but they are nonetheless important. Indeed, until this century, when the novel nearly replaced poetry as the most challenging medium for a writer, few English novelists display anything like the curve of development traditionally associated with poets. Almost always, the seeds of the novelist's last works are contained on nearly every page of his first. For a number of reasons, some mechanical, some social, we cannot imagine John Keats as having written novels or achieving his amazing growth if he had written them. Instead, a novelist's growth is usually more restricted and "organic," in a neutral rather than an honorific sense. What was implicit becomes explicit; what was a thematic element becomes an emphasis. In Thackeray's case, at least, there is this "opening out": the exposure of the implicit, the branching off into new emphases, together with the discovery and refinement of artistic techniques that embody the thematic expansion.

If we look for reasons in Thackeray's mind for this development, we probably need no more than the challenge to which being more explicit is always a response. This challenge might be particularly strong in the case of a satirist who has had plenty of targets but has never had to explain very fully the source of his ammunition. It is as though he were asked, "You say life can be best understood—laughed at and sympathized with—from your position? But what is your position, exactly? And more than that, how would you go about proving it to be valid, insofar as artists ever prove anything?" With these questions the next two chapters will be concerned.

Thackeray did not cease to be a satirist, but he does seem to have accepted a responsibility to "build into" his works more of his vision, to embody in characters and their actions more of the assumptions of *Vanity Fair*. Whether or not this change was entirely for the better is a question that will occasionally concern us throughout the rest of this study, but the answer may ultimately rest on preferences we cannot profitably discuss. Some readers will always prefer the dense ambiguities of *Vanity Fair* to what they may consider the unfortunate clarifications and necessary simplifications of the later novels. My own feeling is that more is gained than is lost.

The most obvious change after *Vanity Fair* is the selection of a central character. With only slight variations, Thackeray settled on the device of building his novels around the story of a young man making his way in the world. From Arthur Pendennis to Denis Duval, the hero of his last and unfinished novel, these young men have more similarities than differences, as do their stories. With the character of young Pen, Thackeray apparently found a structural principle that allowed him the freest use of his powers. Starting from this new figure, we may consider some of the thematic implications that the young tyro brought with him, some of the opportunities and responsibilities he offered Thackeray.

THE TYRO

A composite picture of all these young men, of Thackeray's tyro, would sacrifice some of the life in any one manifestation, but such a picture is possible because he is not so much a raw individual (whatever that would be) as the occasion for certain kinds of reflection and certain forms of action. Physically, he is of middle size and neither outstandingly handsome nor frustratingly homely. Socially, he inherits a position in the middle class, though it is largely technical, a matter of externals. Because he must learn to become worthy of his rank, must become a true gentleman, there is sometimes a technical variation in his inheritance which taken literally could produce false pride or false shame, or both. Henry Esmond is both the son of a noble and bears the burden of illegitimacy. Such obstacles can only be overcome by an inner and spiritual assumption of the rank of gentleman.

Many of the tyro's inner characteristics seem to follow the pattern "x but y"—although, as we shall see, such oppositions of characteristics are not always as simple as they seem. He is apt to be generous but proud, or clever but lazy, and part of the purpose of such a pattern is to establish character without relinquishing the sense of his ordinariness. If he is very handsome, like Clive Newcome, he is very vain. Morally, we are often told, he is only so-so; and his claim on our sympathy, we are assured, is not going to be very strong. Yet our interest in him is not supposed to focus on his "adventures," in any mechanical sense, but on what he is and what he becomes.

The invitation to identify with this young fellow, which underlies all his averageness despite the distance we are promised we may retain, is of course a very strong one. But more interesting than such rhetorical matters, and subsuming them, is the fact that he stands at the center of the known world—socially, morally, intellectually—or, if he does not, can at least get there from where he is. At the center is a state of being from which most of life's distinctions are seen to be unimportant and ephemeral. The former tyro has triumphed over enough of his own vanity, over the exclusiveness of his technical betters, and over the dangerous and limiting adhesiveness of his technical inferiors, to the extent that he can speak for all society and all life. In a sense he *is* all society and his success is therefore the partial "redemption" of society. Kenneth Burke's phrase for one aspect of literary works—the "secular prayer"—applies particularly well to these tyro novels because they are secular and not-so-secular "prayers" for the purification of the world. Through the figure of the tyro, Thackeray is ultimately celebrating life on earth as he understands it.

To use such quasi-theological language may seem absurd if it is measured against either Thackeray's announced intentions—a modest firmness in the cause of "truth"—or the "feeling" of reading his books. I shall consider that feeling in the next chapter, which will deal with the extraordinary sense of reality most readers notice. In this chapter, dealing with thematics, we need two initial hypotheses: first, that the reasons for the popularity of a popular writer are often quasi-religious; and, second, that the satisfying feeling of a rich complexity in art may in part be due to very simple causes. Buttons labelled "mystery" and "awe," for example, probably await, in all of us, the proper pressure. However, we need not try to read Thackeray's mind for its conscious or unconscious designs in order to describe the prayerful nature of his novels.

The particular nature of the prayer can only be seen against the nature and career of the tyro. As an occasion for certain kinds of reflections and for certain forms of action, he brings with him possibilities for exploration and exploitation that are both common to his breed and peculiar to Thackeray's view of him. He has a certain amount of history, this tyro, usually related in Thackeray to the questions of how his grandfather made his money and to the love affairs of his parents. In general, Thackeray subscribes to the notion that it takes three generations to make a gentleman, but he does so with the reservation that the process is not at all automatic. If the three generations are recent ones, the odds are slightly better, for the nineteenth century is on the whole a better training ground for gentlemen than any previous century. Again and again, families who are deceived by the externals of gentility are butts, often through the inversion of their own snobbery. The worldly, aristocratic branch of the Newcomes are proud of a fictitious ancestor who was supposedly a *barber* to King Edward the Confessor, and Henry Esmond's stepmother, Lady Castlewood, convicts herself of silliness by her pride in the family's hereditary office of "Warden of the Butteries and Groom of the King's Posset." But more important, the tyro's history is the occasion for reflection on and dramatization of the influence of heredity and environment.

Thackeray is, broadly, an environmentalist, for hereditarians were apt to use their theory to exclude from society those without sufficiently "good blood" while including fools and scoundrels. However, Thackeray typically avoids commitment to a camp and prefers investigation of the question. He casts an understanding but sceptical eye, for instance, at characters who speak of themselves in environmentalist terms, as they are usually doing so in order to excuse themselves for not being better than they are.

The tyro's mixed nature not only proves him representative, but calls for some sort of morphology of characteristics. To Thackeray, what is forgiveable in youth, and even admirable, would be unbearable in middle age; yet simple reformation seems to him to be improbable in life, to be dangerous to our sense of identity in characters, and to be a view most often proposed by canting hypocrites. Accordingly, the process of improvement is one of refinement rather than change, which explains why the "x but y" pattern of characteristics is not so simple as it looks. Even vanity, or pride, can be made use of in later life, and is not so much the opposite of virtue as a crude and characteristically young form of what may become independent manliness, for instance, when those around one are "toadies" and "tufthunters."

Yet the identity of the self, a question, as we shall see, that interests Thackeray, requires some unchanged dross at the end of the progress and bears testimony to man's fallen condition. Moreover, in his eyes, the doctrine of human perfectability is not only absurd but dangerous, as it is only through a sense of the necessity of human limitations that we learn sympathy and charity.

By definition the tyro is young and dependent. Because he has not been taught yet to lie or to cover up his emotions, he is "fresh" and "honest" and "artless." Because he is dependent, he has a keen eye for kindness; and correctly, in Thackeray's view, he essentializes the world into the kind, the unkind, and a range of intermediate characters who only pretend to be kind or are kind when it costs them nothing or would be kind if they were not so worldly, and so forth. The thematic oppositions to kindness were part of the Victorian novelist's stock in trade, and Thackeray makes full but characteristic use of the possibilities surrounding that favorite figure of contemporary novelists, the orphan. It is as characteristic that he usually does not destroy *both* parents as it is that his narrator seems to take a distant view of the youngster's essentializing in remarks on the naïveté of the little tyke who has not learned much of the world yet. The distance is of course largely ironic, and the satire is directed not at the tyro but at adults and, rhetorically, at the hypothetical reader.

Thackeray may have avoided orphans because most children are not parentless, but more important than statistics is that most children, luckily, have a mother. The existence of tyros almost automatically requires teachers, especially for a quasi-environmentalist, but lucky indeed is the boy with a pure woman for a mother: perhaps second in importance only to the existence of the tyro is the appearance in these later novels of mother-figures. They play too important a part to be discussed yet, and may figure now simply as one of those competing teachers who make up most of the tyro's environment and who allow Thackeray to play competing views of life against one another, both outside and inside the mind of his major figure. None of these figures is a Hans Castorp and none of these novels is Thomas Mann's *The Magic Mountain*. But Clive Newcome, for instance, "took his coloring" from those around him, and built into the plan of all of these novels is some of the same concern that Mann displays for the relations, in his tyro, between raw materials and development under the tutelage of carefully relevant teachers. Major Pendennis, for instance, in order to end the Fotheringay affair, not only consciously plays on Pen's existing family pride and vanity, he *is* Family Pride and Vanity.

As a central figure, and a young one, the tyro puts at the center of the novel what we may call desire. In the case of most novelists, one would hesitate to point this out, but for Thackeray the centrality of desire is both a change and a major part of his vision. *Vanity Fair* was crowded with assorted people, with assorted wants, but most of these wants were seen as selfish designs for foolish objects. But from now on, the histories of his major characters are going to be organized around their desires; and, were these characters to cease wanting—as Pendennis and Henry Esmond and Clive Newcome all nearly do—they would be sinning against themselves and life as a whole. That wisdom, as well as identity, begins in desire and can never leave it behind is one of the keys to Thackeray's vision, and simple as it sounds, it will fit many locks. There is, for instance, the constant pathos found in youthful "freshness," which may be described as a capacity for enthusiastic attachment, if only to cakes and tips at school. The pathos is connected not only with the quixotism of youth, its confusion of illusion and reality, but also with our alleged middle-aged inability to "feel." In Matthew Arnold's poetry, the fear of sterility of feeling is connected with such public and historical causes as the loss of religious faith, rather than with Thackeray's more private and "timeless" explanation of the ordinary encroachment of selfishness. But, as I shall argue, this fear is ultimately connected to religion as fully in Thackeray as in Arnold.

Desire, too, has other uses. Among them is the ability to establish the "otherness" of the world, as measured by its resistance to desire. This opposition is, of course, nothing new in Thackeray, but it is more noticeable and central because of the tyro's centrality. Linked here are the questions of Fate and religious belief, and opportunities for the exercise of such moral qualities as bravery, persistence and constancy, humility, performance of painful duties, and selflessness. Indeed, all of Thackeray's favorite virtues are called into play by the frustration of desire, a pattern which of course did not escape him, and which increasingly struck him as religiously significant.

With a slight darkening of the novels after *Pendennis,* produced by the increasing opposition of the world, comes a compensating insistence on various sorts of transcendental victory over the world of time. Timelessness had always been connected to Thackeray's ideas of virtue (Colonel Dobbin was admirable not least for his constancy) but there is an increasing emphasis on, and recurrence of, the timeless that culminates in Colonel Newcome's dying word, "Adsum!" ("Present!" or "Here!"). Compared to *The Newcomes,* the earlier *Pendennis* is a relatively happy book, showing the world full of prizes of the sort that the seekers themselves desired. "The Ordainer of the Lottery," in the narrator's closing remarks, seems a relatively sympathetic deity. But in *The Newcomes,* the announcement of Clive's marriage to Ethel is reserved for a mocking postscript, which relegates the question of Clive's temporal happiness to "Fable-Land," where everyone is allowed his heart's desire. In the story itself, the prizes include a great many "blessed griefs," a position that is probably better theology and that also marks a slight shift in Thackeray's emphases, as though he had become more aware of the transcendental nature of his morality.

By putting the tyro at the center of these novels, then, Thackeray undertakes to describe a process seen retrospectively—both the process and the retrospection raising questions about the significance of time—and sets himself the problem of designing a significant curve of growth in one character. Where that character begins, what the stages are in his growth, what growth itself turns out to be toward—these are questions that are brought suddenly to the center of the stage instead of being distributed about eccentrically in the panorama of *Vanity Fair.*

THE CURVE OF ACTION

To speak of action, or plot, in the typical Thackeray novel presents certain difficulties. We have seen him apologize for the lack of "art" in *Pendennis,* and the narrator of *The Newcomes* says at one point:

This narrative, as the . . . reader no doubt is aware, is written maturely and at ease, long after the voyage is over whereof it recounts the adventures and perils; the winds adverse and favourable; the storms, shoals, shipwrecks, islands, and so forth, which Clive Newcome met in his early journey in life. In such a history events follow each other without necessarily having a connection with one another. One ship crosses another ship, and, after a visit from one captain to his comrade, they sail away each on his course.[1]

The elaborate metaphor of the voyage, which is pursued even further than I have quoted, is too complacent for real apology; and its artificiality should not prevent our seeing the very strong claim being made to verisimilitude. "Such is life," the narrator is saying; and no apology for plotlessness is really necessary. In fact, the apology in the preface to *Pendennis* goes on to link plots to artificially and meaningless fictional conventions.

Perhaps the lovers of "excitement" may care to know, that this book began with a very precise plan, which was entirely put aside. Ladies and gentlemen, you were to have been treated and the writer's and publisher's pocket benefited, by the recital of the most active horrors. . . . The "exciting" plan was laid aside (with a very honourable forbearance on the part of the publishers) because, on attempting it, I found that I failed from want of experience of my subject; and never having been intimate with any convict in my life, and the manners of ruffians and gaol-birds being quite unfamiliar to me, the idea of entering into competition with M. Eugene Sue was abandoned.[2]

Plots are not only conventional and unreal, then, but concern murder and other large-scale crimes. Thackeray is joking, but the joke is recurrent and varied enough to point to his assessment not only of his own material, the "ordinary" complexities of middle-class life, but also of the mechanical connection between events that he consciously avoids.

Yet the pains he took with *Henry Esmond* (waiting to publish it until it was finished rather than plunging into serialization while writing it) suggest that his apology for lack of "art" was in part serious, and that some technical notion of progression and culmination seemed to him an idea worth breaking, for at least once, his ordinary habits of composition. Nevertheless, except for the saturation in historical detail, which alone might have made concentration seem necessary, and the symmetrical division of the novel into three books treating roughly the hero's boyhood, youth, and early manhood, the "plot" of *Henry Esmond* is more similar to that of *Pendennis* than it is different. There is the same conscious, seeming disjunction of events, the apparently arbitrary crossing and recrossing of ship's courses that the narrator of *The Newcomes* feels to be like real life. More important, if we take "plot" to mean not "machination" but "that which culminates in fulfillment," *all* of the books after *Vanity Fair* have something very much like the same "plot"—which, to avoid confusion, we shall call the "curve of action."

After *Henry Esmond,* Thackeray went back to serializing, and he did so, I venture to guess, not out of laziness or a sense of defeat, but out of a sense that the gains made possible by a sharper focus on a single character's "history" were not essential to the kind of art he had in mind. His next novel, *The Newcomes,* is as broad as *Vanity Fair.* As in that book, we follow two tyros, Clive and Ethel, who in this case appear on different branches of a large and complicated family tree, and who figure only slightly in the first sixth of the book. Yet it is not the recurrent motif of "marriages of convenience" that holds all this material together, but a curve of action similar to that of *Henry Esmond* and, *mutatis mutandis,* of *Pendennis.*

All three novels—to limit ourselves to the three next in time and popularity to *Vanity Fair*—have happy endings. And though we have seen Thackeray prefiguring Henry James' amusement over the ritual bestowal of awards and prizes at the end of novels, we should beware of dismissing the fact, as both authors seem to do, as being no more than a mere popular convention. For one thing, conventions are never completely empty of meaning, as the common phrase "mere convention" mistakenly implies, and for another, no convention need be used automatically and arbitrarily. Thackeray and James, in their strictures on the convention, are measuring it against a sense of life we might call partly statistical (life is not a bowl of cherries, and novelists ought not to say it is), but this argument, though important to their sense of calling, is open to rejoinder by someone with a different set of statistics, like William Dean Howells. Aesthetically, the only problem with a happy ending is the requirement that it be a real ending, a culmination, so that fulfillment and not authorial interposition seems to take place. Thackeray obviously had this sense in mind, and consciously or not made increasingly rich use of a pattern of culmination which we may term "The Seeming Defeat." Seen as a defeat, some event is the end of a *sequence* of attempt; but its illusory quality of sorrow covers a real victory that has been preparing all along.

One startling example is the penultimate ending—the "first" ending—of *Henry Esmond*. The hero has been pursuing, in the third book of the novel, a scheme to restore the throne to the Stuarts. Involved for him in this scheme is his family's historic loyalty; his own devotion to his earliest teachers and benefactors, who were Jacobites; the exercise of his own force and resolution when all around him are wavering, which is a value in itself, like the use of his sword arm; and his long love for Beatrix, whom he hopes to impress, despite her repeated refusals of marriage. Against his own despair of winning her, he must struggle or die. It is a nearly hopeless task that he has set himself: can he, a simpler romancer might have asked, snatch victory from the very jaws of defeat? No, says Thackeray. Riding back to London a few hours too late, Esmond sees the crowds and hears the trumpets announcing the death of Queen Anne and the ascension of the Young Pretender's rival, George I. "With that music," says Esmond, "the drama of my own life was ended."[3]

But during the prosecution of this scheme, a counter-movement, hinging on discoveries Esmond makes, has been developing. First, the prince for whom this scheme is designed turns out to be weak and self-indulgent, unlikely to make a good king. Second, Esmond is troubled at discovering his own selfishness in linking private hopes for Beatrix with so moment-ously public a matter. Third, all politics come to seem arbitrary and meaningless, although the opposition's theory of kingship seems slightly better than his own because more democratic. And, finally, Beatrix, who carries a life of flirtation and worldly ambition to the edge of active vice, is clearly unworthy of his long devotion. By a process of paring away, of repudiations culminating in Esmond's burning the documents that linked him through wealth and titles to the social system for which he has been fighting, he stands in the London crowd a gentleman alone, the only true victim and victor in all that noise. In a fuss of activity, his has been the only truly significant action, we are to feel, though mere external action has been an inappropriate expression of his inner triumph and vindication. It is not that he has snatched victory from defeat, in the romancer's phrase, but that he has found victory shining there in the midst of seeming defeat. England can hope only to catch up with him. The only appropriate external embodiment of this victory is the final realization of love in Rachel, a love "immeasurably above all ambition, more precious than wealth, more noble than name."[4]

This second ending, apt to trouble modern readers who fail to see any necessary connection between the first and second endings, may be partially defended on the grounds of its narrative as well as moral "inwardness." Rachel's love for Esmond and his devotion to her have simply "been there" for two thirds of the book, and so fit the pattern of seeming defeat. Her love has itself been etherially purified of selfishness and jealousy through a sequence of scrupulous guilt and self-immolation. By repudiations similar to Esmond's, she has attained the purity of maternal devotion. At least, we may say, like calls to like, and the abstract patterns of their experiences match.

This large curve of action has been prepared for and paralleled by smaller ones, which have generally taken the form of vindication: either the inner vindication of the knowledge of one's virtue amid unjust accusations, or the outward vindication of big scenes in which Esmond's right to title and property is revealed to those who think him a bastard. Because they confuse virtue with rank, they are sufficiently overmatched by the news of his real station; they are then stunned with admiration by the knowledge that he has repudiated that level of life by leaving the title in the name of his cousin and has risen to the higher one of generosity and loyalty.

These patterns of vindication and seeming defeat may appear to be appropriate to a Victorian version of the *perfect* gentleman, but less appropriate to the "ordinary" tyro described in the last section. My account has, of course, omitted Thackeray's range of devices intended to make his model believable, if not ordinary, but in one sense the virtues expressed in the patterns we have been noting constitute Esmond's primary claim to being "ordinary." Based as they are on what Thackeray considers the simple truth of emotions as opposed to the devious illusions of politics and ambition, Esmond's virtues are recommended as the very opposite of the extraordinary.

Still, Arthur Pendennis and Clive Newcome must get along with less certainty than Esmond, and their route to his simplicity is longer, less successful and, we may decide, more interesting. They know less to start with, and less in the end, perhaps because their problems of identity—though less dramatic than Esmond's Hegelian progress from bastard to viscount to gentleman—are a great deal more complicated. Instead of the hopeful crowning scheme that carries its disillusioning lessons, moreover, they struggle with disillusion itself, and must become disillusioned with disillusion.

But one would do no great injustice to their stories to find, initially, a curve of action describable as a series of defeats resulting in victory. Broadly, Thackeray designs in these novels a transformation of desire that must be carefully progressive at the same time that it loses none of the paradoxical force to be gained from the sudden moment of seeming defeat. In *Pendennis,* we find a mounting series of seeming defeats that result in the happiest of them all: Pen, finally jilted by Blanche, is free to marry Laura. In *The Newcomes,* the pattern is darkened, and the element of defeat in the seeming defeat is more positive and painful, though not triumphant.

By then, Thackeray seems willing to say, victory is possible only through defeat, so central has the pattern become to his view of life. The differences between the two books point to the quality of abstractness in patterns such as this one, though this pattern is nevertheless not simply empty, waiting for any use whatever that happens to cross Thackeray's mind. *Pendennis* is largely "about" the problem of personal identity, whereas *The Newcomes* concerns itself with the more general problem of worldliness and unworldliness. But these questions are for Thackeray so closely related that his uses of the pattern of seeming defeat are never far apart.

What is at stake in the moment of seeming defeat ordinarily involves both identity and unworldiness, and the pattern is appropriate to both purposes for it allows the display of abiding truth amid the wreck of appearances. Truth may emphasize the identity of a character or the existence of "unworldly" virtue, but the difference is apt to be one of emphasis only. In a wonderful scene in *Pendennis,* Lady Rockminster tells Pen, who has been politely smirking as he undergoes her eccentric but searching examination of his plans, "You are very glad, and you are very sorry. What does it matter, sir, whether you are very glad or very sorry? A young man who prefers Miss Amory to Miss Bell has no business to be sorry or glad."[5]

Such a young man evidently cannot be said to exist, not only publicly ("What does it matter?") but internally. Because his emotions are meaningless, he might as well give up having them. Is this a matter of personal identity, or of "unworldliness"? Thackeray would agree with his dowager to the extent that his tyros have to learn to be worthy of having emotions. Valuable as any "sincere" emotion is, the process of growth is the transformation of mere desire into love; and only at that stage can the tyro be said to know who he is.

The role of defeat in this process of transformation is interesting principally in two ways. To be a process at all, to be progressive, each occasion of defeat must be in some sense cumulative. Diagramatically, we should get not a linear progression but a branching figure in which each defeated alternative, each lopped-off branch of defeat, is an appropriate outgrowth of a previous occasion in which defeat figures. But what immeasurably enriches this design is the fact that defeat itself—disillusion—becomes one of the stages in the process and, as stated earlier, must be itself defeated.

Pendennis shows this progress most neatly. The first half of the book consists of a series of adventures that all seem to end—do end, in Pen's eyes—relatively badly. He is defeated in his pursuit of Emily Fotheringay, defeated in his consequent college career as a worldly-wise and gentlemanly man of parts, defeated in the adventure consequent on that defeat when Laura rejects his first offer of marriage. Thereupon Pen elects to settle down, and to cut his losses by adjusting to his defeats. Having become a self-supporting author, he intends to marry Blanche Amory, accept the seat in Parliament that her step-father will provide, and "grow up." This period of seeming success, and its promise of future extension, draws not only on plot elements from previous adventures (the verses he wrote as a boy, his debating successes in college), but on their thematic transformation: the verses had been passionate, though bad, whereas he now writes gracefully and casually; several versions of gentlemanliness, from the youthful hero to the college man of parts, had been tried, and he is now willing to use the notion externally to trade on the snobbery of publishers. His youthful passion for the Fotheringay has become material in a popular romance. Each of the previous episodes, then, has contributed some passion that has become a skill, some intensity that has become largely externalized.

Thackeray is at his best in making this period of adjustment not only dramatically believable but very nearly the proper response to the life presented in the novel. A brief infatuation with the lower-class Fanny is presented as being in part an unconscious revulsion from so passionless a life, but the interlude only reinforces a sad sense in Pen of social ranks and duties, marking a further definition of his identity and of what it means to be a gentleman—a role unfortunately he now cannot escape, he realizes, without being "false" to himself. Moreover, the adjustment is not completely passionless, the externalization not complete, because of the pervasive tone of sweet sadness in his manner. This is the period when the long-delayed knowledge of self-limitations flowers, if that is not too exuberant a word for this movement toward self-knowledge and toward the charity that self-knowledge makes possible.

So many of the previous episodes have turned on illusions about himself or the objects of his desire that Pen's growing clarity is a functioning resolution of previous tensions. To turn this resolution inside out, as Thackeray now proceeds to do, may seem on one level like the double ending of *Henry Esmond,* as though Pen were granted all this growth and Laura too. There is, to be sure, more than a note of comic opera in the ending here, which is deliberately comic and happy, and the young lovers even spend the last chapter arranging the lesser but material happiness of other young lovers. The relation, however, between Pen's final happiness and his period of adjustment is, if anything, more closely designed than that of the two endings of *Henry Esmond.*

After the repeated shock of collapsing illusions, Pen has grown to underestimate life, to leave out of account its highest values. But there is a higher plane of "underestimating" life, through resignation and renunciation, which Pen's mother had known all about and which he must experience before he can rightfully estimate life. Pen's sweet sadness, as it turns out, has been premature, derived from the repeated loss of mere illusions. Only when he can give up his truest desire will he have earned the right to the view of life he had assumed. There is accordingly the countermovement toward a scene perhaps indebted to a different kind of opera, in which Pen's friend Warrington, Laura, and Pen himself resign, in turn, their hopes for bliss. Warrington loves Laura, but is hopelessly married, and so tells Pen that Blanche's history frees him of any gentlemanly obligation to carry out his engagement to her, for Warrington knows that Pen would propose to Laura if free of Blanche. Laura, who loves Pen, advises him to keep his promise to marry Blanche, and Pen chooses Laura's advice. Because this scene re-enacts the frustrated love affair between Laura's father and Pen's mother, both of whom are now dead, the ultimate decision here is "otherworldly" in the extreme. This is the most serious form of the seeming defeat in the book, as each character in turn testifies to the transcendental and objective nature of generosity and love in the midst of the wreck of his hopes.

The merely mock defeat of Pen's jilting by Blanche, and his subsequent reward in marriage to Laura, underlines the inadequacy of Pen's earlier estimate of life without essentially changing it. On one level, life turns out to be happier than he had dreamed possible, but on another level he has merely penetrated to the realm of transcendental passion, inhabited chiefly by mothers. This passion alone holds together and dignifies for Thackeray the sweetly sad view of life's limitations that Pen had held earlier.

If it seems paradoxical to call this main curve of action a countermovement, it is nevertheless a way of describing something very much like a paradox. Surrounding Pen's growth in the last half of the book are those schemes and counterschemes that involve the Claverings, Major Pendennis, Captain Altamount, and Morgan the butler. It is the paradox of high comedy that all this activity should rise, teeter, and topple of its own weight while Pen escapes unhurt. But more important—as we saw in *Henry Esmond,* where the comedy was much less exuberant and Jonsonian—this double movement is the key to Thackeray's conduct of action.

Some of the thematic reasons for his uses of this pattern have been suggested here, and there are, of course, others. On the simply moralistic level, for instance, defeats are taken to be victories if they chasten the egotistic self who knows nothing of life but its own desires. Though Thackeray uses this notion occasionally, it is too simply hopeful to fit his sense of life and too linearly sequential for his sense of structure. Chastening requires, that is, defeat followed by some sort of awakening. *Pendennis* uses this sequence, all right, but it is not enough in itself to complete the action. Closer to Thackeray's sense of life and of comedy as well is the moment that is both defeat and victory. In *Pendennis,* accordingly, he builds toward the serious moment of victory in defeat, as in the big resignation scene or the comic moment of defeat in victory when Pen discovers the ludicrous Harry Foker engaging in awkward but welcome love-play with the faithless Blanche.

THE NEWCOMES

With this pattern of ambivalence in mind, we are in a better position to understand Thackeray's last great novel, *The Newcomes.* For otherwise, how are we to describe the curve of action in a book that seems to focus finally on the lives of two young tyros, Clive and Ethel, but that has spent nearly half of its length before Clive becomes very much interested in Ethel? One way out of the difficulty would be to give up the idea of action entirely and consider the book a picture of society, with no more design than *Vanity Fair's* rudimentary parallels between Becky and Amelia. Or similarly, noting that the title names a family, and that most of its members make marriages of convenience, we might narrow and thematize the definition by describing the book as a treatment of certain specific social problems that were favorites of Thackeray.

Yet the scene at Colonel Newcome's deathbed, as the book ends, does not figure in the "treatment" of "problems," but as the culmination of action. Nothing more is necessary, which may be one of the reasons for the relegation of further detail to the postscript. By various thematic routes, all the major characters are meant to have arrived at this scene united in their ability to participate in Colonel Newcome's final moment of triumph over the world. Looking backward over the novel from this point, we can more easily see the relations among the stories of the three main characters—the Colonel and the two tyros—as well as some of the reasons for the arrangement of the action.

What has happened is that the moment of seeming defeat, the key to the conduct of action in the previous novels, has been raised to the level of explicit subject matter. "Quixotism" we may call this subject, for Thackeray evidently thought of this book as being heavily indebted to *Don Quixote*. There is something unhappy in our doing so because the subject and resulting book are so unlike that of Cervantes. But Thackeray's fondness for *Don Quixote* and his own implicit practice apparently brought him to a highly conscious attempt to design a book that would deal with the fortunes as well as with the necessity of quixotism in his own times. The first third of the book accordingly establishes, through the figure of Colonel Newcome, the existence of quixotism, and the remaining two thirds follows the Colonel's attempts to live out that position as the two tyros undergo initiation into it.

Clive's education, much like Pen's, moves through a series of seeming defeats into defeat itself and out the other side; Ethel's education moves through a series of seeming successes into renunciation and out into love. The Colonel himself is interesting because, aside from presenting the background against which the contributing subplots make sense, he must himself come to terms with his own quixotism. All three characters, we are to feel, arrive at his deathbed with but a single mind, a single view of life, as the book ends.

Colonel Newcome is quixotic in part because so many characters in the book think of him that way. He was called Don Quixote in India, and even Clive "would have blushed for his father's simplicity" but for his own "fine sense of humor." The Colonel has an old coat, hopelessly outdated, which in a flash of sanity and humility he decides to replace, and quaintly old-fashioned notions about the proper distinctions between social ranks, which he never quite sheds. In the first two extended scenes, he defends the ideal of sexual purity, first by scolding a group of songsters and later by launching into an imaginary castigation of Fielding's character Tom Jones. Of the two scenes, the second comes a little closer to Cervantes, as when his harangue is interrupted by the entrance of a real-life servant to whom he tries, in the ensuing confusion, to apologize. But rarely does his quixotism draw on the rich interplay of illusion and reality we associate with Cervantes; even in this scene the Colonel is not significantly confused but merely divided between the fierce "idealism" of his contempt for Tom Jones and his sympathy for actual servants.

The first scene, when Clive and the Colonel visit a pub, is more typical. Firmly set in an atmosphere of nostalgia, it is preceded by the narrator's reminiscence of the fresher, more zestful times of his own youth, when this scene occurred and when the very songs in the pubs seemed brighter and happier.

There is a still purer freshness, however, in the Colonel's "artless" anger against one of the songs, and his subsequent tirade leaves behind in the pub a chastened "company of scared bacchanalians."[6] His quixotism, it turns out, consists not in the conflict of truthful illusions beset by false realities, but rather in certain virtues which we are to take as wholly admirable, and to which he does his simple best to make the world conform. The primary interplay is accordingly not between illusion and reality, but between virtue and failure. It is a curious pattern, involving finally a peculiar kind of triumph over desire, but so self-evident does Thackeray find its meaning that even the children at the school where the Colonel is dying have heard "the noble old gentleman's touching history," and have "all got to know and love him."[7] Looking back over his history, we may wonder what they made of it, for its meaning resides in its partial failure.

It is probably no accident that, as a widower, the Colonel is both father and mother to Clive, for he shares with Thackeray's best mothers the fact that his primary virtues are his affections—for old friends and relatives—and his nature consists in simply having these affections and holding to them, despite opposing circumstances. Indeed, without the opposition of circumstances he would be neither motherly nor "quixotic," in Thackeray's meaning of the term; and he is never more in danger of losing his true identity than in his few brushes with success. His dream of coming home from India to live with Clive was meaningful only as an existing dream, its own excuse for being, and he begins to waste away in the actuality of the dream's realization.

Still attempting to fit external circumstances to a similar dream, he tries to use his new wealth to buy Ethel's hand in marriage for Clive; and, when foiled, he enters politics in revenge against her brother Barnes. There his affections for the Crown, the poor, and the rich leave him unsuited for articulating his views—indeed, for having any "views" at all. But, what is worse, he wins the election. Luckily for his nature he loses his wealth in the failure of his company, and can resign so external a role as member of Parliament. He has meanwhile arranged the marriage between Clive and Rosey, the last and most damaging of his successes. Only as a pensioner at his old school, poor and solitary but beloved and offered money which he can refuse, does he find the momentary balance between success and failure that has eluded him, that defines quixotism for Thackeray, and is its own reward. Baldly put, the Colonel triumphs over desire while still enjoying the desire; his is the triumph of not having one's cake but of nonetheless eating it. Thackeray conceives of this moment not so much as a personal triumph, however (for the Colonel to be conscious of his state, for instance, would be out of the question), but as an objective event in the world's history, one in a timeless order of beautiful moments.

Indeed, the significance of these events for Thackeray is primarily religious. After seeing the Colonel among the other pensioners, for example, the narrator asks, "And who that saw him then, and knew him and loved him as I did—who would not have humbled his own heart, and breathed his inward prayer, confessing and adoring the Divine Will, which ordains these trials, these triumphs, these humiliations, these blessed griefs, this crowning Love?"[8] And speaking of Mme. de Florac, whom the narrator and his wife "loved because she was like our mother," he says: "I see in such women—the good and pure, the patient and faithful, the tried and meek—the followers of Him whose earthly life was divinely sad and tender."[9]

Mothers and other quixotics "prove God by love" for

Thackeray, as his narrator had said of Pen's mother. That is to say, they "prove" His existence, by nearly the same argument that Tennyson used in *In Memoriam*—the analogy from the persistence of love to the belief in a realm of timeless, all-encompassing Love. Both writers are drawing on popular theology, but both show special emphases: Tennyson, by combining the argument with the notion of transformation, so that love and grief not only persist but are "all changed"; Thackeray, by emphasizing, more strongly in *The Newcomes* than earlier, the pathos inherent in the moment that is both defeat and victory. Ultimately, the pathos of the moment seems to derive from the fact that its pattern strikes Thackeray as Christlike.

From this angle, "worldliness" in his novels can be seen to serve two different purposes. The group of characters that includes Barnes Newcome and Lady Kew helps by simple negation to define the "unworldly" nature of love. But at a deeper level, any desire at all figures for Thackeray as worldly, perhaps because it must be located in the existing self and must have mundane objects. Without this sense, Colonel Newcome's reduction to poverty and loneliness could hardly figure as losses, and his dying wishes for Clive and Leonore would only be forgiveable errors. A mother's prayers have only "*something* of Heaven in them" (my italics), a Principle, as it were, in a necessarily human form. And even a Lady Kew must be partly exonerated by the act of desiring what she believes, however mistakenly, is best for Ethel. By a kind of sleight of hand, these two notions of worldliness link all the characters in a Thackeray novel together. The "lesson" of his thematic action, then, is that to desire is human; to desire quixotically, generously and in the midst of defeat, divine.

Chapter Six

LATER FICTION: THE SENTIMENT OF REALITY

REALISM AND EXPERIENCE

"What is it that gives one," wrote a typical reader of *Vanity Fair*, "such a sense of life lived"[1] within the covers of a Thackeray novel? Thackeray himself had mentioned his desire to convey as much as possible of the "sentiment of reality,"[2] and admiring readers since his day have registered the same baffled response, tackled the same question in very much the same terms as his phrase implies. Starting from the reader's sense of reality, his "sentiment," to what can we point to account for it?

Several strategies have seemed useful. By placing the difficult question of reader response on the more manageable ground of literary history, we can speak of the rise of "realism" in the novel, try to define it in either its risen or genetic form, and then hope to place Thackeray at some point along the line of development. The critic is—or used to be—saved thereby from sounding naïvely limited and from seeming to speak too generally about effects that might proceed from totally different kinds of work. After all, this approach reminds us, "realism," unless very carefully and antiseptically used, is an honorific term; and the writer who sets out to be realistic undertakes above all to be persuasive. It is therefore only prudent to neutralize the problem and to accept the very real challenge to discriminate the realism of Thackeray from that of Fielding, or Jane Austen, or Henry James. Primary assumptions would be that literature is an institution—that no work simply springs into being—and that one can therefore best "see" Thackeray by placing him against Fielding, and looking ahead to George Eliot or Proust. Praise, in this context, would be strongest for his innovations and mildest for the traditional things he simply does well; his failings can be handled very tolerantly, and may be more than made up for by the debts of later writers to him. Much of the best criticism of the last two centuries has been at least closely related to this position. But in the case of Thackeray, the most valuable criticism has usually avoided the question of realism altogether, or spirited it in under those allegations of wisdom that we have already considered. Such terms as realism, it has often been felt, belong to manifesto writers and anthologists, not to the discriminators of literary continuity and achievement.

Yet there was something, René Wellek has cogently argued, in mid-century England and Europe that deserves to be isolated as an historical event. Writers thought of themselves as doing something new that they called Realism; moreover, they actually produced works that have some relation to their announced intentions. The distinguishing features, Mr. Wellek decides, are an often unconscious confusion of description with prescription; of "the objective representation of contemporary social reality" with didacticism, reformism.[3] The confusion of the two sides can be accounted for, he implies, by the fact that "the theory of realism is ultimately bad aesthetics" for "all art is 'making' and is a world in itself of illusion and symbolic forms."[4] True, or at least one of the assumptions of this book. Although Mr. Wellek calls his definition a "disconcertingly trivial conclusion,"[5] it is one that not only still needs to be made, but that also provides a basis for extension and discrimination.

In discussing *Vanity Fair,* I spoke of a contrast between two modes of thought and expression in that work, designated "realism" and "satire," distinguishable by whether or not the moral values involved were presumed to be discoverable within experience or were imported from outside. The curve of action described in the last chapter is a good example of Thackeray's attempt to embody values in the experience of his characters, to have values waiting there, as it were, to be discovered. Yet the resonance of that moment of culmination was, as we saw, by analogy religious—each character could "prove God by love"—and to that extent alone, setting aside the strong inheritance of eighteenth-century satire, Thackeray belongs on any historical scale prior to George Eliot and Henry James.

George Eliot, to be sure, invests the natural order of her world with many of the emotions and terms of the religious one (an experience of Dorothea Brooke's "cost her a litany of pictured sorrows"),[6] but not in order to analogize between two orders. Religious experience had become for her, as for Ludwig Feuerbach, an intensely important and significant *human* experience, so that her religious "borrowings" are not really borrowings at all but signs for her of the underlying continuity of human experience between an older age of faith and the present skeptical one. With so much at stake, so much to be discovered in experience, she is in effect driven to the exercise of that moral intelligence which F. R. Leavis and others so prize. By means of her belief in that faculty she is able to construct a more or less consistent world. Both her characters and those of James have a great deal to learn, but they not only have that curious faculty enabling them to know, they can be sure that all they need to know is out there in experience, waiting to be learned. Some of their characters, especially of James', do not learn, and are doomed, like Winterbourne in *Daisy Miller,* to remain what they were. But the pathos of their doom depends on their having missed their chance, of having been among those on whom something important was lost. The chance was always there.

The case of Ethel Newcome's awakening is a good one to set against the next two generations. When Ethel discovers the pointlessness of her life and refuses Lord Farintosh, Laura Pendennis is moved to some characteristic reflections on the nature and value of experience; and, to a large extent, she seems to be speaking for her creator:

> "Do you know," [she asks her husband,] "there are many points that she has never thought of—I would say problems that she has to work out for herself, only you, Pen, do not like us poor ignorant women to use such a learned word as problems? Life and experience force things upon her mind which others learn from their parents or those who educate them, but for which she has never had any teachers. . . . [There follows a diatribe against the teachers she *has* had, who raised her for the marriage market.] Ethel's simple talk made me smile sometimes, do you know, and her *strenuous* way of imparting her discoveries. I thought of the shepherd boy who made a watch, and found on taking it into town how very many watches there were, and how much better than his. But the poor child has had to make hers for herself, such as it is; and indeed is employed now in working on it.[7]

The operating cause of the difference here between Thackeray and his great followers is his loyalty to his reformist theme—I have omitted a great deal of Laura's invective against the marriage market and its (logically necessary) effects on the young. We are always being taught something, Laura implies;

and, for want of better guides, we will be taught by worse. All the pathos of the mistreated orphan lies behind the attack on the ill effects of society. This indignation is possible because experience is not claimed to be continuous, in the manner of George Eliot or Henry James; instead, it is conceived to be composed of discrete categories, morally tagged and ranked. Something called "experience" is laboriously overcoming something called "teaching," a distinction that by the time of James will have almost disappeared.

Even allowing for the fact that Laura is to some extent a character, a mixture of the well-brought-up English miss and the domestic angel pointing upward, Laura speaks here for Thackeray,[8] whose loyalty to even so limited a concept of experience is hedged and selective. To the moral intelligence, the epistemological half of the later realism, must be ascribed two important characteristics: first, centrality within the personality; and second, the power of organizing experience "meaningfully" by leading the self into an appropriate relation to the world "out there." Thackeray could make neither of these claims.

Yet there is another kind of "continuity of experience" very much on his mind, if not in his bones somewhere: the sense of character present in all the forms that the self takes. After Ethel's conversion, for instance, she throws herself into the High Church line with almost as much imperiousness and rigidity as she had shown in her days of empty triumph. Some passages in a letter from Ethel to Laura show that Thackeray's hand for parody, far from having lost its skill, kept finding new uses for its craft. "What a fright," she writes, "you must have had with my little god-daughter! Thank Heaven she is well now and restored to you. You and your husband I know do not think it essential; but I do, *most essential,* and am very grateful that she was taken to church before her illness."[9] This rather fierce Diana, as Clive had once called her, now has new game to hunt: "Little Barnes comes on bravely with his Latin; and Mr. Whitestock, *a most excellent and valuable* person in this place, where there is so much Romanism and Dissent, speaks highly of him."[10]

But the real danger—or beauty—of her conversion lies not simply in the politics of religion now available to her, but in her temptation to think of herself in these crude new terms while ignoring such facts as her brother's dishonesty. "Hard, selfish, worldly, I own my brother to be, and pray Heaven to amend him; but dishonest! and to be so maligned by the person [Laura] one loves best in the world! This is a hard trial. I pray a proud heart may be bettered by it."[11] Much of this letter is concerned, explicitly and implicitly, with the nature and value of experience.

Ethel wonders, for instance, whether some people are simply unable to "comprehend a world beyond" as she had been unable to understand art until Clive taught her; and she even wonders, what is theologically even more dangerous, whether the "secret of all secrets, the secret of the other life" may be "unrevealed to some."[12] Her contemporaries would be quick to notice the untutored nature of her reflections, and perhaps be moved to agree with Laura's condescension toward the insufficiency and even dangers of merely personal experience in matters of such grave import. But good readers would also notice that Ethel's speculations stem from a growing habit of sympathizing, that the play of her tentative ideas here is really only the form that her sympathizing takes.

There is thus a difference for Thackeray between "experience" regarded as a result and opposable to "teaching," and "experiencing," seen as a process, the favorite example of which for him is the activity of sympathizing. Experience is not the best teacher, but experiencing—especially the vicarious sort that is sympathizing—may well be. Considered intellectually, as a "position," this notion perhaps more than any other helps distinguish Thackeray's world from Fielding's or even Jane Austen's relatively more stable and consistent worlds of Good Sense. Seen experientially against the more ambitiously monistic worlds of George Eliot and Henry James, Thackeray's world can seem only a rudimentary and partial version of theirs. Certainly in other ways, especially in the subtlety of problems conceived, it is.

But in this matter of the inherent treatment of experiencing, Thackeray's world can stand against theirs as a more skeptical and perhaps even more interesting one. Ethel's letter is a triumph, partly because its satiric and approving elements do not easily add up. We are driven to entertain the sense of a mind—and, more than mind, a sort of energy of self-hood—reaching out through speculation and dogma which, we see, both imprison and liberate, although the continuity between Ethel's new and former self remains unbroken. The lessons that George Eliot's narrator might draw from such a character—the need for sympathy on a large scale, for enjoyment mixed with pathos in our contemplation of one another—are all present but implicit. And, even better, they are partly enunciated by Ethel herself, forcing us to see in our subject a limited and therefore "human" version of the point.

A theory of literary realism, then, even one so "disconcertingly trivial" as Mr. Wellek's, does provide one way into the problem we began with: to account for the sense of so much life lived. For out of a writer's sense of what experience is like, and of what it offers, proceeds a good part of that projected "life lived."

THE FORMS OF EXPERIENCE

More fundamental to our sense of the "life lived" in a novel is the matter of structure, which is why formalist criticism is never ultimately so bloodless as its opponents suppose. For example, Jerome Thale, discussing matters highly relevant to Thackeray, strikes the note of approving scrutiny most typical of recent criticism in dealing with the problem of structure in Trollope. Form in Trollope, Thale says, derives not from conventional plot but from an intricate pattern of "parallels, contrasts, repetitions, and slight variations." A Trollope novel is "like a vast mural, one of those comprehensive images that cover walls, crammed with figures and united spatially."[13] But Thale's argument extends beyond the parallel with murals to our sense of embodied life, for he claims that "structure is the grounds of significance . . . the means through which Trollope's wonderful disenchanted clarity of vision, his tolerance and accuracy, operate to produce a remarkably complex and balanced vision of human life."[14] We are used to hearing that structure embodies a writer's vision, but Mr. Thale seems to be saying something else, something even more difficult to isolate than "vision."

Perhaps the point—an important one for understanding Thackeray—can be made more simply and neutrally by noticing that when we respond with a very strong sense of the lifelike to what we feel, for instance, is a "special case," we are at least subliminally taking in two sorts of information at once: the notion of what an ordinary case is like, and the notions that distinguish the particular one from its kind. The sense of the lifelike evidently depends very heavily on the interrelations between such different sorts of notions, assuming that both exist strongly enough for superimposition to occur without blurring. Much of Thackeray's art depends on the double notion of the special case and of related configurations. To account for the *sense* of life in his novels we must move from life itself into matters of form.

For, to take the example of the special case, art in the novel differs from life to the extent that both the norm and the variation, the idea of case and that of specialness, are contained within the work. Rudimentary satire, or an ordinary joke that makes fun of someone, tends to set the absurd deviation against an unexpressed norm that is socially held and therefore needless to spell out. But Thackeray is not simply the satirist Hippolyte Taine and his followers saw: a novelist spoiled by his propensity for satire. He is a comic artist, who presents both norm and deviation in wonderfully complex and diverse ways.

In a recent book John Loofbourow discusses some of the literary modes that Thackeray manipulates.[15] Chivalric romance, fashionable fiction, and epic, Mr. Loofbourow claims, are for Thackeray's plots and characters modes of action and belief—belief in the way things go, norms of possibility. In *Vanity Fair,* Mr. Loofbourow sees these norms as the expressive forms of neurotic compulsions in the characters. Amelia, seen from without, is the victim of fashionable sentiment and motherhood, an imprisoning set of mind-forged manacles. These neuroses add up to relativism for Thackeray, to a world seen ultimately as a mere collection of subjective worlds. *Henry Esmond,* on the other hand, is true epic of a new sort, and in it Thackeray manages to construct an objective world to which his characters' subjectivism can be meaningfully related.

Mr. Loofbourow's argument overstates the differences between the books by discounting as simply subjective many notions that seemed partially or completely objective to Thackeray. Yet his is the kind of argument for which the criticism of Thackeray has been waiting. Perhaps we can start further back, prior to definable modes, or at least labels, from the loose and general notion of the special case.

The existence of some sort of rigidity is central to Thackeray's continual emphasis upon the special case, both structurally and thematically. The seeming defeats we have considered are defeats with a difference. *Vanity Fair* is a novel without an ordinary hero; and Thackeray's plots, to the extent that he uses them, are always a special version of plots that exist not only as ideal literary forms outside the novels but as expectations held by characters within the covers. Clive's love for Ethel, for example, takes surprisingly long to begin, and he marries someone else during the course of it. Yet these variations surprise not only the expectant reader of novels but characters such as Colonel Newcome and even the narrator.

The variations exist against what is probably the strongest sense of convention in English fiction. Jane Austen, the nearest parallel to Thackeray, discovered as early as *Northanger Abbey* a double usefulness in literary conventions: her heroine must not only outgrow her amusingly Gothic expectations but must discover "real life" versions of the Cruel Father, the Rescuing Lover, the True Friend. Similarly in *Pride and Prejudice,* but with a widened mastery, it is not only a truth universally *held* that a single man in possession of a fortune must be in want of a wife, as the book's first sentence satirically asserts, it is also happily, luckily true—with important and saving differences. The pleasure of such survivals, such restatements in other keys, is the pleasure of the vaudevillean "double take" compounded by one more reversal. "These youngsters will of course marry?" "No, not a chance, the world being what it is, and they being who they are." "But look!"

The first reversal is of course persuasively "realistic," a

simple example of the special case, but it is surprising how often the second seems realistic as well, when there has been a real modulation into a second and perhaps even a third key. In part, I suppose, our sense of reality here depends on synthesis, where the final affirmation is also a reaffirmation: "marriages *are* made in Heaven, after all, but in a real Heaven, for use upon this earth by people like us."

Mr. Levin's definition of literary realism, the correction of x by y,[16] stops too soon to account for Thackeray or Jane Austen, perhaps because fewer of the Continental works he wanted to emphasize return on themselves in the way so many of the great English ones do. Or such a culminating drawing together could be considered "merely" a matter of art, of structure seen aesthetically by the sympathetic or of commercial requirements seen contemptuously by the critical.

But just as the seeming defeats are more than mere "effects," such endings are more than simply tacked on, and they are also more than an aesthetically pleasing rounding off that satisfies our desire for "form." To take a more lauded example, in *The Portrait of A Lady,* Isabel Archer's final immersion into "life"—after her initial search for just that element, and her subsequent sense of having settled for precisely its opposite—would be meaningless except as the culmination of that total three-stage progression. And there is a strong sense in which "meaningfulness" there is the same as our sense of "realism." For example, were Isabel to run off, at the end of the book, with Caspar Goodwood, the frustration of the good reader would amount to a sense of unreality, for so much that had been "at stake" would have been allowed simply to evaporate.

Rigid and inadequate as the thesis stage is in such a pattern, it is the necessary ground for development because it presents the matters at issue in a version that will be not simply corrected but rather restated. In considering Thackeray's ubiquitous uses of patterns and variations, then, we shall have to avoid Mr. Loofbourow's tendency to regard the patterns as merely confining. If Major Pendennis, for instance, were simply "wrong" about marriage, merely the pathetic prisoner of his own mundane shrewdness, he would be a much less useful character in *Pendennis* than he is. And he would be much less "real," a proposition the reader can test by imagining him in the work of any other writer. Even among Thackeray's works, it is only in *Pendennis* that the Major could be caught up and most fully used, and that his characteristics could resonate with the fullness for which we often reserve the word "real." And, as the example of the Major may remind us, the three-stage pattern of thesis-antithesis-synthesis, though certainly present in Thackeray, is not fundamental. The kinds of internal dynamics it allows us to consider, however, are.

That three-stage pattern can be seen as a special variety of the special case, for in its reaffirmation it simply adds one more reversal. Another very common variety is the result of inadequate alternatives, as when Colonel Newcome and Barnes are both wrong about the sort of life Clive is leading in London. The Colonel is sure that Clive is working very hard at his painting; Barnes, that he is going to the devil.[17] Thackeray, who need hardly make the point that the truth lies somewhere in-between, is therefore free to concentrate on the matters of character implicit in the three main actors in the little drama—Clive's real nature, the Colonel's naïve fondness, Barnes' suave enmity—as well as in a number of other minor figures such as young Moss, Mr. Binnie, J. J. Ridley, the allegorical Jones and Harry, and their mothers and friends.

The effect of such richness is not relativistic for two reasons: the overly rigid alternatives define very clearly the general area in which the truth is to be found; and the ancillary figures help define the mixture of criticism and indulgence appropriate to the case of this "poor young rogue." Examples of such self-convicting rigidities occur everywhere in Thackeray, and range from local issues like this one down to the smallest passing remark ("poor young rogue") and up to the opposition of large-scale attitudes that shape the plot (like Pen's first romantic view of love and his uncle's shrewd reduction of it). "It does not follow that all men are honest because they are poor," says the narrator after the opening fable of *The Newcomes,* "and I have known some who were friendly and generous, although they had plenty of money. There are some great landlords who do not grind down their tenants; there are actually bishops who are not hypocrites; there are liberal men even among the Whigs, and the Radicals themselves are not all Aristocrats at heart. But who ever heard of giving the Moral before the Fable?"[18]

Much of "the moral," as well as of the artistry, no doubt does lie in these self-convicting rigidities; although, for reasons we considered in discussing *Vanity Fair,* when "morals" are explicitly at stake Thackeray is at least as apt to "essentialize" to some sort of heart's truth, or to lament the loss of a simpler view. On his last rueful trip to Blanche, Pen envies both priests and priest-haters, although such alienation is a stage in the thematic pattern of progress toward seeming defeat that we considered in the last chapter. More central to Thackeray's thinking about rigidity is an extraordinary conversation between Pen and Laura a few chapters earlier.

> "I think for some of you there has been no fall," he said, looking at the charming girl with an almost paternal glance of admiration. "You can't help having sweet thoughts, and doing good actions. Dear creature! they are the flowers which you bear."

> "And what else, sir?" asked Laura. "I see a sneer coming over your face. What is it? Why does it come, to drive all the good thoughts away?"
>
> "A sneer, is there? I was thinking, my dear, that nature in making you so good and loving did very well; but—"
>
> "But what? What is that wicked but? and why are you always calling it up?"
>
> "But will come in spite of us. But is reflection. But is the sceptic's familiar, with whom he has made a compact; and if he forgets it, and indulges in happy day-dreams, or building of air-castles, or listens to sweet music let us say, or to the bells ringing to church, But taps at the door, and says, 'Master, I am here. You are my master, but I am yours. Go where you will you can't travel without me. I will whisper to you when you are on your knees at church. I will be at your marriage pillow. I will sit down at your table with your children. I will be behind your death-bed curtain.' That is what But is," Pen said.
>
> "Pen, you frighten me," cried Laura.
>
> ". . . Didn't I say," he added fondly, "that some of you seem exempt from the fall? Love you know, but knowledge of evil is kept from you."[19]

Like Thackeray's American contemporary, Hawthorne, Pen speaks as though it were goodness that was always simple, evil complex, or at least the complicating factor—a division that prevents both Thackeray and Hawthorne from subscribing wholeheartedly to the nineteenth-century extension of the Fortunate Fall, whereby the "fall" into experience is a necessary step in the soul's education. For Thackeray and Hawthorne, the knowledge of evil is an evil in itself; but fascination with the complex is central to both writers. Like Hawthorne's Hilda, of *The Marble Faun,* Laura is admirable but incomplete. We might perhaps choose her simplification of the world if we had the choice, but unfortunately we do not. And even in so morally freighted a discussion, there is a clear note of satisfaction in not being "allowed" such pleasing simplifications. The farther the distance from explicit morality, the greater the satisfaction.

Another common configuration deserves mention. Perhaps the most frequently noted, it might be called "the overlay" and is an event that recurs in the life of a character or perhaps a family. Gordon Ray mentions a fine example in *Vanity Fair*: the moment when young George Osborne discovers in his father's boyhood room, after he himself has been living there, his own initials. " 'Look here, mother,' said Georgy, 'here's a G. O. scratched on the glass with a diamond; I never saw it before, *I* never did it.' " "By a hundred unobtrusive touches," says Mr. Ray, "Thackeray reminds us that, as time passes, the cycle of life repeats itself."[20] Such touches do that, as well as accomplish a number of other things, in almost endless variety and combination. Sometimes they point to the bitterness of time having passed, as in the widowed Amelia's part in Mr. Ray's example, or in Pen's revisiting his boyhood home, or in Clive's listening to speeches, after his marriage, in the same room with the now unattainable Ethel. Sometimes they provide emotional distance comically, as when Pen, who finds Mr. Bows slaving for a new protégé in whom Pen has interest, is forced to compare this new temptation with his earlier infatuation for Emily Costigan.

We may be tempted to say that an event, especially in these later novels, is no sooner established as "true," as happening, than we may begin to expect some more or less emphatic recurrence, an overlay of either parallel or parodic force. We have discussed the long, frustrated, but time-softened passion of Pen's mother and Laura's father, and its parallel near the end of the book, when the next generation rises to the same experience. But there have been other parallels in Pen's two infatuations and Blanche Amory's lachrymose pretenses that are summed up in her volume of poems, *Mes Larmes*. These events and attitudes are "measured," with more or less severity, by the standards established in the first occurrence of the pattern. Such occurrences, as in the arranged marriages of *The Newcomes,* define each other in ways that become clearer in considering an extended example.

PENDENNIS

Although Thackeray apologized for the "lack of art" in *Pendennis* as a whole, the book opens with a section of sixteen chapters that make a unit as controlled and sustained as anything he ever wrote. Almost a novelette, it deals with Pen's life up to his departure for Oxbridge, and, like a novelette, this section has a center of focus—his infatuation with Emily Costigan—around which are deployed an astonishing variety of relevances that act as echoes, mostly mocking ones, to the central "note."

Even his handling of the narrative line shows a greater concern for careful management than does *Vanity Fair*'s relatively sprawling shape. The opening chapter, in which the Major receives at his club the letters from his nephew and sister-in-law, beautifully prepares not only for five chapters of flashback within flashback, but, by providing the initial thematic materials, for the complexities to follow. These letters of appeal intrude into a world in which the Major is accustomed, among other comforts, to "neat little confidential notes, conveying female entreaties,"[21] not to such real agitation as his sister-in-law's; he is used to dining with the nobility, not to hearing such "noble" sentiments as his nephew prides himself on displaying. ("A delay implies a doubt," writes Pendennis, "which I cast from me as unworthy.")[22]

This triple contrast raises with great mastery and *efficiency,* as it were, many of the interlocking thematic issues of the book. In contrast with the widowed mother's appeal, the Major's life is made to seem superficial and habitual—a style of life rather than, in an as yet undefined way, life itself. Some sort of reality principle inheres in her letter, which the Major must grudgingly acknowledge. Whatever that principle is, however, it as clearly does not belong to his nephew's letter, which is dated at "Fair Oaks, Monday, Midnight," that Byronic hour, although "written in a great floundering boy's hand." This letter is a masterpiece of self-imposed humbug, the more wonderful for claiming to penetrate such obfuscations as "the present prejudices of society" and his mother's alleged provinciality, though swallowing whole the legends of his family's and Emily's noble lineage: "When our ancestor, Ralph Pendennis, landed with Richard II in Ireland, my Emily's forefathers were kings of that country. I have the information from Mr. Costigan, who, like yourself, is a military man."[23] Such a tissue of conventions is this young man's view of himself—man of feeling, lover "fated" to know but one "passion" in life, gentleman honor-bound to abide by his vows, smug male condescending to protect the tremulous "woman who loves me fondly," man of the world and shrewd judge of character—that the Major's frustrated "rage and horror" on reading it seem almost appropriate. His reaction comically is not appropriate, of course, for on the scale of agitation that Thackeray has established he falls much nearer his nephew's position than his sister-in-law's. "My nephew marry a tragedy queen! Gracious mercy, people will laugh at me so that I shall not dare show my head."[24] More precisely, the scale of comparison has to do with the relation between a constant—agitation, by the principle of synecdoche a stand-in for the self—and the formal terms by which one lives. Young Pendennis lives almost entirely in his borrowed forms, the Major on relatively equal terms with them (unlike Captain Costigan, for instance, he is in fact a real major), and Mrs. Pendennis lives in the fairly unformalized role of worried mother. This is Thackeray's great subject, the relation of the self to forms, but he is here moving beyond *The Book of Snobs* and *Vanity Fair* as though trying to address himself more seriously to the double question of the relation of the self to forms, and of these to life.

By encompassing the two letters within the Major's experience, then, Thackeray has begun with a formal density rare even for him. The Major will be able to act as a standard of objectivity against which Pen's more delusive fancies can be measured; but already we know of realms of experience closed to the Major, some of which have to do with the very conventions Pen has borrowed. And in terms of the organizing question raised, he himself is only another object lesson, a special case. For what hold these characters together, and what make each of them a special case, are their individual relations to some organizing form of life and the relation of that form to reality. Two working definitions of form quickly emerge: first, form as a subjective projection of self-delighting order onto life; and, second, form as a prepared convention that exists prior to the self's transactions with it. In the second chapter, the process by which Pen's father sets about becoming a gentlemanly country squire is an example of the latter, and his mother's excessive pride in her family an example of the former.

But neither of these forms is ever presented unmodified by some relation to another kind of reality. Absurd in many ways as he is, Pen's father does have some of the qualities formulated in the role of gentleman; and his mother's projection of excellence onto her son and husband is the counterpart of her own real excellence as wife and mother.[25] A double perspective is thus required, which will enable us to see the form in relation both to the self and to external reality.

With Pen, the case is even more complicated. By the end of the second chapter he already combines the two kinds of formal errors his parents have made, as when after his father's death he imagines himself suddenly become the gentleman his father had been and imagines that role as ludicrously powerful, as a kingly "reign."[26] But, so far, there is almost no relation to life at all. Instead of moving from experience into a formal role, like his father, or projecting meanings from one side of experience onto another, like his mother, Pen is in the position of living by pure formulation, and he soon becomes aware of the inadequate occasions for expenditure of all this mental energy. Like Don Quixote, he "used to ride out, day after day, in quest of Dulcinea."[27] And as with Cervantes, Thackeray's point is not simply the satiric concern with the distance between formulation and reality, but the richly conscious artistic concern with the interplay among self, form, and fact. For this reason, Thackeray can make brilliant use of what would otherwise be merely satiric materials.

His young Quixote at the theater, for instance, before his first sight of Emily, hears the opening scene of von Kotzebue's sentimental drama, *The Stranger,* in which the hero's servant sums up his master's life. It is an existence strangely—and comically—parallel to Pen's: "Again reading," says the servant, "thus it is, from morn to night. To him nature has no beauty—life no charm. For three years I have never seen him smile. . . . Nothing diverts him. Oh, if he would but attach himself to any living thing, were it an animal—for something man must love."[28]

We are reminded that the conventions Pen had so glibly marshalled, in his letter to his uncle, were not irrelevant to the thematic action of even the first chapter and are becoming more relevant to Pen's existence throughout these flashback chapters. The narrator tries to explain the force of this play, crudely written and monstrously overacted though it is.

Those who know the play of the "Stranger" are aware that the remarks made by the various characters are not valuable in themselves, either for their sound sense, their novelty of observation, or their poetic fancy.

Nobody ever talked so. If we meet idiots in life, as will happen, it is a great mercy that they do not use such absurdly fine words. The Stranger's talk is sham, like the book he reads, and the hair he wears, and the diamond ring he makes play with—but, in the midst of the balderdash there runs that reality of love, children, and forgiveness of wrong, which will be listened to wherever it is preached, and sets all the world sympathising.[29]

Perhaps the narrator is right, and the whole world is set sympathising, but Pen's relation to this "balderdash" is more direct and immediate than that of Thackeray's "world" seems to be—unless we take "sympathizing" to be a rather transitory effect. More complex and appropriate is the reaction of the musician Bows to the gestures and intonations he himself has taught Emily, the Fotheringay: "When she came to this passage little Bows buried his face in his blue cotton handkerchief, after crying out 'Bravo.' "[30] Evidently there are no conventions totally irrelevant to the experience of these characters; knowing all he does about the "real" Emily Costigan and her complete ignorance of the role he has taught her to play does nothing to lessen the force of the presented form on Bows' loveless life.

A charming and pathetic touch by itself, this one-sentence gesture of Bows, in the Cervantesque realm in which Thackeray is working, is also highly resonant. There is no escaping the appeal of forms, Thackeray seems to say. The major question is how much of internal and external life they organize and give expression to. After seeing Emily act, Pen is sure that he is "as much in love as the best hero in the best romance he ever read"[31]—but he is also really in love, if only with the expressive form of "Love and Genius," which "seemed to look out from [her eyes] and then retire coyly, as if ashamed to have been seen at the lattice."[32] An intricate analogy between Pen's first love affair and his first watch shows Thackeray thinking about both kinds of "usefulness," the inner and outer, but the emphasis seems to fall on the external usefulness of an accurate account of time:

> The boy took [the watch] from under his pillow and examined on the instant of waking: forever rubbing and polishing it up in private and retiring into corners to listen to its ticking: so the young man exulted over his new delight; felt in his waistcoat pocket to see that it was safe; wound it up at nights, and at the very first moment of waking hugged it and looked at it.—By the way, that first watch of Pen's was a showy, ill-manufactured piece: it never went well from the beginning, and was always getting out of order. And after putting it aside into a drawer and forgetting it for some time, he swopped it finally away for a more useful timekeeper.[33]

But we must be careful to avoid reading a simple satirical intent—simply measuring idea against reality—into such remarks, or even into such apparently simplifying juxtapositions as that between Pen's exalted thoughts on his ride home from first meeting Emily and her casual remarks to her father about the number of tickets the young man will probably take.[34] In isolation, such a juxtaposition might seem to oppose exalted delusion to crass vulgarity, but it follows and grows out of a more complicated scene in which at least four main elements are in play together. There is his love, ennobling the object; her commonplace world of the weather and a pie sent out to the baker's; her stunningly majestic beauty; and her equally real simplicity and good humor. No element, polarizing the world into value and disvalue, is more important than the others. The point is simply that these elements do not add up but are all in motion, as it were, at once.

Pen's image of himself as an heroic lover, subsuming all the literary and social models he most wants to emulate, and its projection onto the heroically beloved Emily, are of course vulnerable to factors that seem to be "real," if only by their power over his formulation. He does not have the money of a prince, a fact which his princess and her father will take seriously; and lack of money here stands for his more general lack of power to coerce the world into a proper shape. Moreover, his princess is nearly illiterate, and the secret of her ghost-written letters to him looms, we know, as a threat to his formulation.

More interestingly, the Major's campaign to flatter him into conceiving of himself in some higher role, to which Emily would be a hindrance, "places" his present order on what seems to be the wider field of a superior order. He begins to see around his present role by measuring it against another—one that is not more "real," but simply functions as though it were. More subtly still, Pen feels himself observed, in the presence of the Major and of his valet, Mr. Morgan, as though for the first time he is moving in a world too large to be coerced: "Nothing was said at home. The lad seemed to have every decent liberty; and yet he felt himself dimly watched and guarded, and that there were eyes upon him even in the presence of his Dulcinea."[35]

The end of it measures but does not make sense of Pen's great affair. So far *Pendennis* is much like *Vanity Fair,* although more precise and interconnected. But, in addition, two new stories frame Pen's major one, and reflect upon it. Just as Pen is beginning to suffer in love, we hear the story of his mother's early love for Laura's father, Francis Bell, a tale of mutual and serious suffering that contrasts with Pen's relatively imaginary throes. Their love affair had been frustrated by Bell's prior engagement to a vengeful spinster who refused to set him free and whom, in the name of honor, he foolishly married. Pen in the name of honor will refuse to entertain doubts about Emily. But the earlier love affair is a story not only of greater love, and greater suffering, but also of the transforming power of time. Pen's mother married, instead, Pendennis and, as we have seen, grew to worship him. When Bell's wife died, he married again, this time "a colonial lady, whom he loved fondly,"[36] and who became Laura's mother. Time, however, has not erased but has rather transformed that early devotion: Mrs. Pendennis still has a lock of Bell's hair in her desk, and Laura, on the death of her parents, was sent by her father to Fair Oaks, the ward and near-daughter of Mrs. Pendennis. Brief as it is, the story is of major importance because it includes elements missing in Pen's own—a deeper relation of the self to the form of passion, and of that passion to the world symbolized by marriage, career, and the passage of time. For these reasons, the love itself can remain a constant, a line back down through the passage of time, proved real by its capacity for survival and transformation.

The other contrasting and parallel story is that of the sentimental curate Smirke's growing and hopeless passion for Mrs. Pendennis. Smirke is a loosely organized collection of "decent" scholarship, romantic foppishness, and social ambition—all of which are, of course, perfectly sincere. At the height of his self-confidence about his relations with Pen's mother, he exerts all his powers of conversation to please her, talking in a mannner both clerical and worldly, about the fancy Bazaar, and the Great Missionary Meeting, about the last new novel, and the Bishop's excellent sermon—about the fashionable parties in London, an account of which he read in the newspapers—in fine, he neglected no art, by which a College divine who has both sprightly and serious talents, a taste for the genteel, an irreproachable conduct, and a susceptible heart, will try and make himself agreeable to the person on whom he has fixed his affections.[37]

As a counterpart to Pen, that is, he exists almost entirely within a mode, whose primary relation is not to the self, as in Pen's case, but to the outside world. We would say he almost does not exist, or that he lives to please, confident that the mode he has chosen ought to please.

Consequently, Pen's most liberating moment in this section of the book comes near its end when a drunken Mr. Smirke finally confesses to Pen the identity of his mysterious beloved:

"My mother!" cried out Arthur. . . . "Pooh! dammit, Smirke, you must be mad—she's seven or eight years older than you are."

"Did *you* find that an objection?" cried Smirke piteously, and alluding, of course, to the elderly subject of Pen's own passion.

The lad felt the hint, and blushed quite red. "The cases are not similar, Smirke. . . . A man may forget his own rank and elevate any woman to it; but allow me to say our positions are quite different."[38]

Pen's priggishness here is one of those rich moments in Thackeray that sum up and bring together much of the action, partly because it is an inadequate reaction to his feelings. The incident sums up the element of family pride and social rank that has loomed so large in his father's, the Major's, and his own formulations; but Pen only retreats to the position from an initial one of shocked perception of mismatching, physical as much as anything else, and his sense of the involvement of social rank certainly locates something important in Smirke's motives. But the scene is much wider than this. Pen sympathizes with Smirke before sending him off, and from his previous Byronic gloom has suddenly passed, as a result of the scene, to an unexplained cheerfulness. When his mother asks why Smirke has left before tea, Pen "looked at her with a kind humour beaming in his eyes: 'Smirke is unwell,' he said with a laugh. For a long while Helen had not seen the boy looking so cheerful. He put his arm round her waist, and walked her up and down the walk in front of the house. Laura began to drub on the drawing-room window and nod and laugh from it."[39]

The laughter will sound cruelly snobbish unless we hear in it as well the freedom Pen evidently feels for the first time: a sense of his own identity that proceeds from both his ability to see himself in the unfortunate Smirke and his having used responsible power as the actual man in an actual house, which is now once again drawn together for the first time since his father's death.

This achievement is a momentary pause in the novel, but a defining one. It is unstable, because Pen is not his own father, nor his mother's husband, and the element of family pride is still too mechanically operative. As though to emphasize its brevity, Thackeray has Pen return to longing for his lost Emily in the short interval before leaving for the university. But although this section is not a novel in itself, it shows us with what extraordinary intensity and inventiveness Thackeray had put to work his love of parallels and contrasts in the service of his abiding interest in the formal organizations of the self. One concern, I suppose, could be called "method," and the other "theme." They are firmly held together in this section of the book and in this scene in which Pen suddenly seems to understand what it means to see oneself as "a special case."

The book is larger than this section, not only in size but in its thematic dimensions. Where we feel it largest is where it is most repetitive, not where the plot provides new intricacies but where we find new overlays and parallels. This complexity is perhaps what we mean by narrative "intricacy" itself, and a good part of what we feel to be "realism."

CONCLUSION

Much of this book has been thematic in concern, partly because any appreciation of Thackeray today requires a full look at the worst: we cannot make him into a better or more modern thinker than he was. As a man he was brave, rueful, funny, and self-pitying. Much of his life, when he was not writing, was a series of absurd love affairs: for his pretty little wife, who went insane; for the pretty little wife of his best friend, Mrs. Brookfield; and for a pretty little American girl, Sarah Baxter. As early as 1836 a letter to his wife-to-be, scolding her for sexual timidity, contains most of the later love-morality: he has offered her "a love of which any woman in the world should have been proud" and she has shrunk from it in the name of Decorum.[40] The outcome of that marriage, and the following hopeless attachments, reinforced this propensity to a vaguely neo-Platonic belief in Love, and coincided with matters discussed here in Chapters Four and Five such as the form-essence pattern and the moment of seeming defeat.

But just as, in life, he could back off from his suffering, see around it, so his works extend out through these concerns and encompass them. He is at least as much an artist as a Victorian gentleman, and the side of Victorianism that reinforced and applauded his concern with forms is, for our purposes, all to the good. To put it another way, Thackeray is not a case of the artist moving from parody to great art, from the imitation of literature to the imitation of life. He is better than that, more complicated and more interesting. He moves from an interest in the forms that parody makes visible, and their relations to life, to a more generalized interest in the forms which the self uses in life, in an art constructed of parallels and overlays reminiscent of parody. Even his "metaphysics" can finally be seen to contribute to this art, for it encourages the scrutiny of the self and its relations with itself and reality.

That was his true subject, and his achievement consists in our ability to recognize, in so formal an art, the life of the ego in action.

NOTES

The edition of Thackeray used here is *The Complete Works of William Makepeace Thackeray* (New York, 1899; reprint 1903) in 25 vols. References to *Letters* are to *The Letters and Private Papers of William Makepeace Thackeray,* collected and edited by Gordon N. Ray (Cambridge, Mass., 1945–1946), in 4 vols.

INTRODUCTION

1. Kathleen Tillotson, *Novels of the Eighteen-Forties* (London, 1954). See esp. Sec. 9, pp. 33–39.
2. George Eliot, *Middlemarch,* ed. Gordon S. Haight (Boston, 1956), p. 12. It would "do," that is, if the argument confined itself to questions of the morality or immorality of Christianity, as in Francis Newman's *Phases of Faith,* but not if the argument turned, as it did in Strauss and his followers, on matters of epistemology.
3. *Letters,* III, 467.
4. *Ibid.,* IV, 238.
5. *Ibid.,* I, 493.
6. Noel Annan, *Leslie Stephen* (London, 1951), p. 151.
7. *Letters,* I, 213.
8. See, for example, *Letters,* I, 204–206. It was "wrong" principally because the Old Testament was wrong in using the name of God to sanction murder and revenge. "Gothic Xtianity," he called it once *(Letters,* II, 581).
9. *Letters,* III, 20.
10. Annan, *Leslie Stephen,* p. 110.
11. *Letters,* III, 82.
12. J. Y. T. Greig, *Thackeray, a Reconsideration* (London, 1950).
13. Quoted by Gordon N. Ray, *Thackeray,* Vol. II: *The Age of Wisdom* (New York, 1958), p. 425.
14. *Ibid.,* p. 420.

NOTES

CHAPTER ONE

1. *Works,* XXV, 494.
2. *Ibid.*
3. *Ibid.,* p. 496.
4. *Ibid.,* p. 495.
5. *Ibid.,* p. 507.
6. *Ibid.,* p. 504.
7. *Ibid.,* p. 496.
8. *Ibid.,* p. 503.
9. *Ibid.,* p. 499.
10. Harry Levin, *Contexts of Criticism* (Cambridge, Mass., 1957), p. 96.
11. Gordon N. Ray, *Thackeray,* Vol. I: *The Uses of Adversity* (New York, 1955), p. 391.
12. *Works,* XII, 468.
13. *Ibid.*
14. *Ibid.,* p. 476.
15. *Ibid.,* p. 477.
16. *Ibid.,* pp. 478–479
17. *Ibid.,* p. 485.
18. *Ibid.,* p. 486.
19. *Ibid.,* p. 488.
20. In a newspaper review of Disraeli's novel *Coningsby* (13 May 1844), Thackeray did treat Disraeli's vision of the political movement to be called "Young England": "We wish Sir Robert Peel joy of his Young England friends; and, admiring fully the vivid correctness of Mr. Disraeli's description of this great Conservative party, which conserves nothing, which proposes nothing, which resists nothing, which believes nothing: admire still more his conclusion, that out of this nothing a something is to be created, round which England is contentedly to rally, and that we are one day to re-organize faith and reverence round this wretched, tottering, mouldy, clumsy, old idol." Reprinted in *William Makepeace Thackeray: Contributions to The Morning Chronicle,* ed. Gordon N. Ray (Urbana and London, 1966), p. 50.
21. *Works,* XII, 532–533.
22. *Ibid.,* p. 491.
23. *Ibid.*
24. Alexander Welsh, *The Hero of the Waverly Novels* (New Haven, 1963).
25. *Works,* XII, 504–505.
26. *Ibid.,* p. 506.
27. *Ibid.,* p. 533.
28. *Ibid.,* p. 517.
29. *Ibid.,* p. 481. In the *Morning Chronicle* review of *Coningsby,* Thackeray had quoted this passage:

   "I long to see your mare again," said Coningsby. "She seemed to me so beautiful."

   "She is not only of pure race," said the stranger, "but of the highest and rarest breed of Arabia. Her name is 'the Daughter of the Star.' She is a foal of that famous mare which belonged to the prince of the Wahabees; and to possess which, I believe was one of the principal causes of war between that tribe and the Egyptians. The Pacha of Egypt gave her to me, and I would not change her for her statue in pure gold, even carved by Lysippus. Come round to the stable and see her." Ray, ed., *Contributions to The Morning Chronicle,* p. 46.

CHAPTER TWO

1. Quoted by Alan B. Howes, *Yorick and the Critics* (New Haven, 1958), p. 127.
2. See George M. Ridenour, *The Style of Don Juan* (New Haven, 1960), App. B.
3. See esp. Howes, *Yorick and the Critics,* and René Wellek, *A History of Modern Criticism,* Vol. II: *The Romantic Age* (New Haven, 1955). For a suggestive discussion of Horace, see Reuben H. Brower, *Alexander Pope: The Poetry of Allusion* (London, 1959), esp. Chap. 6.
4. *Works,* XIV, 596–597.
5. *Ibid.,* VII, 275.
6. *Ibid.,* V, 127.
7. *Ibid.,* p. 237.
8. *Ibid.,* p. 255.
9. *Ibid.,* p. 249.
10. *Ibid.,* p. 255.
11. *Ibid.,* p. 257.
12. *Ibid.,* p. 258.
13. *Ibid.,* p. 263.
14. *Ibid.,* p. 274; my italics.
15. *Ibid.,* p. 282.
16. *Ibid.,* VI, 337.
17. *Ibid.*
18. *Ibid.,* V, 286.
19. *Ibid.,* p. 275.
20. *Ibid.,* VIII, 519–520.
21. *Ibid.,* p. 648.
22. *Ibid.,* XX, 8–9.
23. *Ibid.,* p. 10.
24. *Ibid.,* VIII, 495.
25. *Ibid.,* pp. 513–514.
26. *Ibid.,* VII, 268.
27. *Ibid.,* p. 207.
28. *Ibid.,* XII, 417.
29. *Ibid.,* p. 380.
30. *Letters,* II, 424.

CHAPTER THREE

1. *Works,* I, 72.
2. *Ibid.,* p. 45.

3. *Ibid.,* p. 78.
4. *Ibid.,* p. 37.
5. Miriam Thrall, *Rebellious Fraser's* (New York, 1934), p. 59.
6. *Works,* I, 174.
7. One may prefer to consider the internal audiences of the book as groups that the reader, as individual, is invited imaginatively to join. Still, the reader in *Vanity Fair,* whom the narrator addresses, is obviously not the reader of the book.
8. *Works,* I, 10–11.
9. Ray, *Thackeray,* Vol. II: *The Age of Wisdom,* p. 427.
10. Leo Spitzer, "Linguistic Perspectivism in *The Don Quijote," Linguistics and Literary History* (Princeton, 1948), p. 72.
11. John Holloway, *The Victorian Sage* (London, 1953; reprint 1965).
12. Kenneth Burke, *Attitudes Toward History,* rev. second ed. (Los Altos, Calif., 1959; reprint 1961), p. 308.
13. John A. Lester, Jr., "Thackeray's Narrative Technique," *PMLA,* LXIX (1954), 392–409; Geoffrey Tillotson, *Thackeray the Novelist* (Cambridge, Eng., 1954).
14. Lester, "Thackeray's Narrative Technique," pp. 400–401.
15. *Ibid.,* p. 406.
16. *Ibid.,* p. 407.
17. Dorothy Van Ghent, *The English Novel: Form and Function* (New York, 1953; reprint 1961), pp. 139–152.
18. *Ibid.,* p. 140.
19. *Ibid.,* p. 142.
20. *Ibid.,* p. 146.
21. *Ibid.,* p. 143.
22. G. Tillotson, *Thackeray the Novelist,* p. 266.

CHAPTER FOUR

1. M. H. Abrams, *The Mirror and The Lamp* (London, 1953; reprint 1958), esp. Chap. 3.
2. *Works,* IV, 615.
3. *Ibid.,* III, 36–37.
4. *Ibid.,* I, 37.
5. *Ibid.,* II, 505–506.
6. *Ibid.,* p. 342.
7. *Ibid.,* I, 269.
8. *Ibid.,* p. 32.
9. *Ibid.,* p. 146.
10. *Ibid.,* p. 49.
11. *Ibid.,* p. 52.
12. *Ibid.,* pp. 169–170.
13. *Ibid.,* p. 181.
14. Charlotte Brontë, *Jane Eyre* (reprint, New York, 1950), p. xxxi.
15. Ray, *Thackeray,* Vol. II: *The Age of Wisdom,* p. 22–23.

16. *Works,* I, 225.
17. Charles Whibley, *William Makepeace Thackeray* (New York, 1903), p. 92.
18. *Works,* I, 27.
19. *Ibid.,* p. 250.
20. *Ibid.,* pp. 37, 170.
21. *Ibid.,* p. 246.
22. *Ibid.,* p. 293.
23. *Letters,* II, 309.
24. His letters provide, as letters will, uncertain evidence of what he thought he was doing. As early as *Catherine* the concept of moral purpose is very strong—the book is meant to make its readers disgusted—but he also thought of it as belonging to the art form of grotesque humor with its own rules to be followed (I, 412, 433). In defending *Vanity Fair,* he used the same arguments, but hedged in the direction of literal truth: *Vanity Fair* is not like life, his project would have been spoiled by including nicer or wiser characters, but at the same time it is probably more like life than we care to admit (II, 423–424). Finally, he became fond of saying that life is better than "some satirists" (meaning himself) "paint it," as though he had all along been thinking of *Vanity Fair* as an equivalent of life (for example, II, 534). In other words, he left his three key terms—purpose, decorum, fidelity—about as confused as he found them, and indeed as they still often are.
25. G. K. Chesterton, *The Victorian Age in Literature* (New York, 1913), p. 29.

CHAPTER FIVE

1. *Works,* XV, 237.
2. *Ibid.,* III, ix–x.
3. *Ibid.,* XIV, 418.
4. *Ibid.,* p. 419.
5. *Ibid.,* IV, 660.
6. *Ibid.,* XV, 12.
7. *Ibid.,* XVI, 801–802.
8. *Ibid.,* p. 763.
9. *Ibid.,* p. 769.

CHAPTER SIX

1. John W. Dodds, ed., *Vanity Fair* (reprint, 1955), p. vii.
2. *Letters,* II, 772.
3. René Wellek, *Concepts of Criticism* (New Haven, 1963), p. 253.
4. *Ibid.,* p. 255.
5. *Ibid.,* p. 252.
6. Eliot, *Middlemarch,* p. 313.
7. *Works,* XVI, 626–627.
8. But see *Letters,* III, 469, where Thackeray agrees with a friendly critic's distaste for Laura.
9. *Works,* XVI, 697.

10. *Ibid.*, p. 699.
11. *Ibid.*, p. 697.
12. *Ibid.*, p. 698.
13. Jerome Thale, "The Problem of Structure in Trollope," *Nineteenth-Century Fiction,* XV (1960), No. 2, p. 149.
14. *Ibid.*, p. 156.
15. John Loofbourow, *Thackeray and the Form of Fiction* (Princeton, 1964).
16. Harry Levin, *The Gates of Horn* (New York, 1963; reprint, 1966), p. 52.
17. *Works,* XV, 184.
18. *Ibid.*, p. 5.
19. *Ibid.*, p. 704.
20. Ray, *Thackeray,* Vol. I: *The Uses of Adversity,* p. 409.
21. *Works,* III, 2.
22. *Ibid.*, p. 4.
23. *Ibid.*
24. *Ibid.*, p. 5.
25. *Ibid.*, p. 14.
26. *Ibid.*, pp. 20–21.
27. *Ibid.*, p. 28.
28. *Ibid.*, p. 34.
29. *Ibid.*, pp. 36–37.
30. *Ibid.*, p. 37.
31. *Ibid.*, p. 39.
32. *Ibid.*, p. 36.
33. *Ibid.*, p. 39.
34. *Ibid.*, p. 51.
35. *Ibid.*, p. 88.
36. *Ibid.*, p. 76.
37. *Ibid.*, p. 145.
38. *Ibid.*, p. 149.
39. *Ibid.*, p. 150.
40. *Letters,* I, 319–320.

WORKS CITED

Abrams, M. H. *The Mirror and The Lamp*. London: Oxford University Press, 1953.

Annan, Noel. *Leslie Stephen*. London: MacGibbon & Kee, 1951.

Brontë, Charlotte. *Jane Eyre*. New York: Rinehart, 1950.

Brower, Reuben. *Alexander Pope: The Poetry of Allusion*. London: Oxford University Press, 1959.

Burke, Kenneth. *Attitudes toward History*. Los Altos, Calif.: Hermes, 1959.

Chesterton, G. K. *The Victorian Age in Literature*. New York: Holt, 1913.

Dodds, John. "Introduction," *Vanity Fair,* pp. v–xviii. New York: Holt, Rinehart & Winston, 1955.

Eliot, George. *Middlemarch,* ed. Gordon S. Haight. Boston: Houghton Mifflin, 1956.

Greig, J. Y. T. *Thackeray, a Reconsideration*. London: Oxford University Press, 1950.

Holloway, John. *The Victorian Sage*. London: Shoe String, 1953.

Howes, Alan B. *Yorick and the Critics*. New Haven: Yale University Press, 1958.

Lester, John A., Jr. "Thackeray's Narrative Technique," *PMLA,* LXIX (June 1954), 392–409.

Levin, Harry. *Contexts of Criticism*. Cambridge, Mass.: Harvard University Press, 1957.

———. *The Gates of Horn*. New York: Oxford University Press, 1963.

Loofbourow, John. *Thackeray and the Form of Fiction*. Princeton: Princeton University Press, 1964.

Ray, Gordon N. *Thackeray*. 2 vols. New York: McGraw-Hill, 1955, 1958.

Ridenour, George M. *The Style of Don Juan*. New Haven: Yale University Press, 1960.

Spitzer, Leo. *Linguistics and Literary History*. Princeton: Princeton University Press, 1948.

WORKS CITED

Thackeray, William Makepeace. *The Complete Works of William Makepeace Thackeray*. 25 vols. New York: Harper & Bros., 1899, 1903.

———. *Contributions to The Morning Chronicle,* ed. Gordon N. Ray..Urbana, Ill.: University of Illinois Press, 1955.

———. *The Letters and Private Papers of William Makepeace Thackeray,* ed. Gordon N. Ray. 4 vols. Cambridge, Mass.: Harvard University Press, 1945–1946.

Thale, Jerome. "The Problem of Structure in Trollope," *Nineteenth-Century Fiction,* XV (Sept. 1960), 147–157.

Thrall, Miriam M. H. *Rebellious Fraser's*. New York: Columbia University Press, 1934.

Tillotson, Geoffrey. *Thackeray the Novelist*. Cambridge, England: Cambridge University Press, 1954.

Tillotson, Kathleen. *Novels of the Eighteen-Forties*. London: Oxford University Press, 1954.

Van Ghent, Dorothy. *The English Novel: Form and Function*. New York: Holt, Rinehart & Winston, 1953.

Wellek, René. *Concepts of Criticism*. New Haven: Yale University Press, 1963.

———. *A History of Modern Criticism,* Vol. II. New Haven: Yale University Press, 1955.

Welsh, Alexander. *The Hero of The Waverly Novels*. New Haven: Yale University Press, 1963.

Whibley, Charles. *William Makepeace Thackeray*. New York: Dodd, Mead, 1903.

INDEX

INDEX